Devotionals From Women to Women

To Inspire, Encourage, & Motivate Women All Around The Globe. Sharing Testimonies of God's Amazing Grace, Unwavering Faithfulness, Everlasting Mercies, And Remarkable Providence.

Compiled By

Dr. Donna Barrett

Devotionals from Women to Women: To Encourage, Inspire, & Motivate Women all Around the Globe

First Printing

ISBN- 978-0-578-99108-5 pbk

Designed & Edited by A2Z Books Publishing Lithonia, GA 30058

www.A2ZBooksPublishing.net

Manufactured in the United States of America.

A Special Gift

Presented to:

From:

Date:

"For I know the thoughts that I think toward you, says the Lord, thoughts of peace and not of evil, to give you a future and a hope." Jeremiah 29:11

Table of Contents

Intro –
Devotional from Women to Women

The thought of sharing testimonials from Women to Women to encourage and inspire them became a robust task during the first few months of the pandemic lock down. *"What can I do to make a positive impact on women?"* was the question on my heart. It wasn't long that the idea of inviting other women to share their own testimony became a reality. I shared the idea with some of my family members and friends and was delighted with their responses.

Women from all over the world began to share with other women and I am glad to announce that 135 testimonials became a reality. This Devotional is about the amazing power of God to intervene at the right time in our lives. From the ultimate gift of life, a stranger donated one of his kidneys to another stranger, to been diagnosed with stage four cancer and is now cancer free, or to receive financial blessings in unfamiliar ways are some of the divine ways the Lord has intervened.

God has done marvelous things for every woman who contributed to this noble task. We are extremely happy to share and bless other women with our testimonies. The global pandemic has caused unprecedented stress, depression, anxiety, and fatigue and sharing our story is one of the ways to inspire women to believe that God is able to do more than they can think or imagine. There may be no glimmer of light at the end of the tunnel, there may be no hope of a brighter future, there may be many obstacles in our path, but be encouraged by Isaiah 43: 2 *"When you pass through the waters, I will be with you, and through the rivers, they shall not overflow you. When you walk through the fire, you shall not be burned. Nor shall the flame scorch you. For I am the Lord your God, the Holy One of Israel, your Savior."*

My sister, I'm convinced God can use our challenges, our heartaches, our crucibles, and our problems to make us stronger and more resilient through the toughest moments of our lives. Nothing is too difficult for God and nothing takes Him by surprise. He is Alfa and Omega, the Beginning and the End, our Sustainer, our Rock, our Shield, and our Deliverer. Let us continue to be faithful through our circumstances knowing He will provide the strength and the courage to carry us through.

As you read these testimonials, may you be captivated anew by the wonderful promises of God.

Be Inspired! Be Encouraged! Be Motivated! Be Blessed!

Dr. Donna Barrett

Sharing Testimonials from Women to Women to Inspire, Encourage and Motivate

This is a unique project, in that, none of these women are paid to share their testimonials. Each sister graciously accepted the invitation to share her experience on how God has intervened and carried her through some of the most difficult times in her life.

Recognizing the difficult times women are experiencing during the pandemic and being aware of God's amazing grace and unwavering faith – we want to share His love with our sisters around the globe.

As we continue to build stronger women – we will build stronger families – stronger churches – stronger schools – stronger communities – and a stronger world. Together we can become agents of change and make the world a better place.

Please support our ministry through Fostering Connections, Inc.:

- Continue to pray for this ministry that we will continue to inspire and encourage other women
- Pledge to support women in homeless shelters and women in distress
- Pledge to support foster care youth aging out of care

Donate via Zelle to – Fosteringconnections2018.com

- One hundred percent (100%) of funds received from sale of "Devotionals from Women to Women" will go to Fostering Connections, Inc. (a non- profit organization) to assist women in distress and women in homeless shelters.

Please contact us:
Dr. Donna Barrett
Phone: 954-483-9280
Email: donna.barrett51@gmail.com

Dr. Maryse Desir
Phone: 954-774-2833
Email: Maryse.desir@yahoo.com

The Ultimate Gift of Life

It was Sunday, December 16, 2018, when I heard a voice, "your granddaughter, Madison should do a video to let the world know that her daddy is in desperate need of a kidney." I listened to the voice and immediately wrote out exactly what Madison should say in the video… "My name is Madison Johnson; I am four years old. My daddy needs a kidney, his blood type is B positive. Please, please, please call my mommy today at *(phone number)*. I texted the message to my daughter, Kameisha. My son-in-law, Delbon, had severe kidney failure and was in desperate need of a kidney transplant. He needed a miracle, he needed God's divine intervention, he needed a donor. We prayed and were assured that God would intervene and do a miracle for Delbon.

Madison created the video with the help of her mom. The video was posted on several social media platforms. In a few days, the video went viral. Subsequently, my daughter received a call from TV Station, CBS46 for an interview. The following week, CNN Headline News, Channel 7 "Help Me Howard" and Google News contacted Kameisha for interviews. After several interviews, they received over 60 phone calls from strangers stating that they would donate one of their kidneys to Delbon. David, one of the potential donors consistently called and texted Kameisha during the process. Throughout the next several months, Kameisha kept saying to me, *"Mom, I think the donor will be David."*

On June 24th, 2019, Delbon received one of the best news of his life, *"Mr. Delbon Johnson, this is the kidney transplant department of Emory hospital, I have some great news for you, we have a perfect match. Your kidney transplant surgery will be on August 26, 2019. Please get yourself prepared for that date."* Delbon was ecstatic! We were happy! We thanked God and prayed earnestly for a successful surgery.

The surgery went well! David and Delbon met one day after the surgery. It was such a special moment for not only Delbon and David, but for both families as well. This is a wonderful experience that I will never forget. God intervened and Delbon experienced the ultimate gift of life. It has been one year and nine months since the surgery. Delbon is recuperating very well, even though he had some challenges shortly after the surgery. We are praising God for His divine intervention and happy to say that he is doing well.

Our situation may look very bleak. It may seem that God is not listening. You may even feel like giving up, but God always comes through on time. Yes, it may not be our timing, but He is on-time. Thank you, Lord, for choosing David to be Delbon's donor! A true blessing, a true miracle, and the ultimate gift of life from God!!

Eternal Father, we praise and magnify Your name for being our Rock and Shield and a very present help in times of trouble. You have kept us in perfect peace while our mind is stayed on You. Thank You for Your divine intervention in choosing David as a donor for Delbon. Bless and keep us according to Your loving kindness and tender mercies. May we continue to talk about the miracle of your abiding presence in our lives. In Jesus Holy name. Amen!

Dr. Donna Barrett

God's Grace

For by grace, you have been saved through faith, and that not of yourselves; it is the gift of God; not of works, lest anyone should boast. Ephesians 2:8,9 (NKJV)

It was a beautiful Thanksgiving morning. My husband and I slept in a little late because neither of us had to go to work. There was a service at church scheduled to begin at 10:00 AM. We had breakfast, got dressed, and as we were heading to the car my husband blurted out, *"wait a minute, I have the keys to open the church doors."* Well suddenly in his mind, we were late, and that is one thing he utterly despised. We hurried into the car and my husband bolted out of the driveway. We maneuvered out of the neighborhood safely and then up the main road which had very little traffic at that time of the morning.

His foot on the gas and his eyes on the road and his watch, the speedometer was left with no one monitoring, then I heard the familiar groan, which alerted me that something was wrong. "Ooooh noooo." I looked up and saw him, too. A police officer came out from his hiding spot behind a clump of bushes and pulled us over. All I could see in my mind's eye was a fat speeding ticket. While my husband was having a conversation with the officer I started to pray. After a very short time, I heard my husband say, *"thank you, officer,"* and we drove off. For the rest of the journey, we did not go a fraction of a mile over 40 mph.

I got to thinking. Isn't that like the grace of God? We commit a sin, we come face to face with God, he pardons us and gives us his beautiful gift of grace which we do not deserve. It would not have been a wise thing for us to continue driving over the speed limit after the police officer gave us grace that morning. In the same way, it is not wise to abuse the grace of God. We should not be doing the same wrong deed repeatedly, but remembering what Jesus did for us at Calvary, we should strive to stay within the limits of the cross.

Everyone at that Thanksgiving service knew what we were thankful for that day. In the same way, we should be sharing with our friends and family what God has done for us and what a joy it is to know that we are not living under the law but within the boundaries of God's love and mercy, and when we get to heaven, we will forever be thankful for God's amazing grace.

Father, we thank you for sending your son to die for our sins and that through his death we can receive your grace which is sufficient for us. Amen.

Sharon Roberts

God's Amazing Grace

So, friend, we can now - without hesitation - walk right up to God, into "the Holy Place." 20 Jesus has cleared the way by the blood of his sacrifice, acting as our priest before God. 21 The "curtain" into God's presence is his body. 22 So let's do it - full of belief, confident that we're presentable inside and out. 23 Let's keep a firm grip on the promises that keep us going. He always keeps his word. Hebrews 10:19-23 (MSG)

God has always been faithful to me during the good and bad parts of my journey, even leading up to me being a Christian. In the times when I wasn't aware that I was lost and needed to be saved, God right there with me. During a conversation with a friend some time ago, I recalled bits and pieces of the past growing up and even some highlights of my life that I shouldn't be quite proud of. I found myself keeping track of certain milestones that would make some people blush; dates that didn't need to be kept.

I am so thankful though that on one fateful day Jesus went on that awful cross for these very blush-worthy milestones, so that they wouldn't be beside my name forever. Since God found me, saved me, and showed me that truth, the truth of what real love is, of what grace is, why would I want to turn away from it. Like

Mary Magdalene, I have many Hicks, but the new milestone memories that have been created with Jesus, far outweigh the ones made in the past. I am grateful that Jesus' sacrifice not only cleansed me but made me perfect and gave me a chance to experience a new and brighter life. Were it not for grace…

Dear most passionate Savior, I am so thankful that I can now call you friend. I am confident in your promises to me that you will never leave me or forsake me, and like You said to Mary that You will not cast stones at me even when the world tends to. I thank You for Your love that surpasses my own understanding. I thank You for Your grace that is so amazing. May the life that I live be pleasing unto You as you have taken me out of darkness and placed me into Your marvelous light. Amen

Kaye Ann Clarke

Trust in His Word

"And it shall come to pass, that before they call, I will answer; and while they are yet speaking, I will hear." Isaiah 65:24

Those who have left their homeland, their families and friends and moved to a strange land will know how that feels, especially if it was not a move that was being planned for a long time but happened rather quickly. When you find yourself in a place where you don't know anyone, unless you are the adventurous type, there is uncertainty and some anxiety. So, let me confess right now that my husband is the adventurous one in the family, not me. He accepted a job on this Caribbean island, and we all moved there. My first daughter however had started college at home, and the plan was for her to remain with the family and finish the year.

As I said before my husband was the one who had a job. I had left my job to move with him, so I was not working at that time except for an occasional substitute teaching position. As a result, we had not yet accumulated savings, so we didn't have enough funds in our recently opened account. However, that situation changed as money would have been transferred from our home account to this new bank account where we were now living.

We were looking forward to our daughter soon joining us, and the time came for us to pay for her ticket. I was preparing to go to the bank to get the money, when I got a call from the principal of a school where I had 'subbed.' She told me that she had a check for me. I could have let my husband collect it since it was the school where he worked, but it was on my way, so I decided to get it.

When I got to the bank, I was confident that we had funds in our account only to discover that our money had not yet been transferred. That could have been a difficult situation, but thank God, I had the government issued check in hand, and I was able to cash it and make the payment.

Little did we know, as I made plans that morning, how God was going to fulfill His promise in His word - "before they call, I will answer." Before we knew that we would have needed that check, He provided it. God's word is sure! We can rest on His promises because His word will come to pass. He will always come through for us not always the way we want, but in His way and His time. I thank God for the many assurances that He gives us in His word.

Father, thank You for the hope, guidance, and assurances that You have given us in Your word. Help us as we continue to study and learn more of You, that we will be strengthened in our relationship with You, in Jesus' name. Amen!

Judith Alexander

The Holy Spirit

"And because ye are sons, God hath sent forth the Spirit of his Son into your hearts, crying, Abba, Father. 7. Wherefore thou art no more a servant, but a son; and if a son, then an heir of God through Christ." Galatians 4:6-7, KJV.

While watching a movie based on history- around the time of the Aztecs. One section grabbed my attention where an elder was speaking around a campfire. There he spoke of how the animals contributed their strength, wisdom, speed, etc. to man because he was sad in his station. But even after all their now added attributes, the owl could still see a great void in man where he will never be satisfied or happy despite taking and taking from those around him. It rang so loudly as truth, even in today's world. We see men of power step on those beneath them continue to gain influence over the world. A world that is not even theirs to claim! Even James, before he was beheaded wrote in James 5 about it as he encouraged those who cried out to God because of the rich man's injustice. He said that "...the coming of the Lord draweth nigh." v.8, KJV.

What brought me full circle was the realization that yes man's carnal heart is never satisfied, but we have a Savior who is willing and able to fill that void. "But God commendeth his love toward us, in that, while we were yet sinners, Christ died for us." Romans: 5:8, KJV. He didn't wait for us to give Him permission to make a way for our sins to be blotted out for us to be able to stand before the Father. Yet, instead of seeking after Him, we try to fill ourselves with the things of this world that will never be enough. They will never satisfy the carnal appetite. "Let him not trust in emptiness, deceiving himself, for emptiness will be his payment." Job 15:31, ESV. "19 Or do you not know that your body is a temple of the Holy Spirit within you, whom you have from God? You are not your own, 20 for you were bought with a price. So, glorify God in your body." 1 Corinthians 6:19-20, ESV.

Dear Jesus, help us not to look to the world to fill the void within us but to look to You who is the author and finisher of our faith. I pray that when we feel empty - as if You have left us - remind us that You promised to never leave us or forsake us, but we must first seek You with our whole being. Thank You for Your filling power, and the fact that it is always available to us. Give us the strength to open our minds and hearts to the Holy Spirit. In Your name, I pray. Amen.

"And ye shall seek me and find me when ye shall search for me with all your heart."

Jeremiah 29:13.

Alexandira Espeut-Thompson

Forgiveness

Carry each other's burdens, and in this way, you will fulfill the law of Christ. Gal. 6:2

"Mother, May I?"

I was convinced I had lost my collective mind. Only a month ago, the anticipation of my mother migrating to the US to stay with me was most exhilarating. I was thrilled that we would finally get a chance to establish a relationship that miles apart had hindered for most of my life. But as I watched her now on the couch, only suppressed memories of failed promises, abandonment and disappointment were engendered. I was gripped by unforgiveness and riddled with resentment. After all, she missed my 14th Birthday after promising she would come. I was sent to Nassau, Bahamas to live with strangers. For two years, I never received a phone call. I deserved to be angry. This feeling was even more amplified whenever she asked for my help with anything.

Jesus! What is this? I know I should love her, but I can't! Silence.

Maybe if I fast, I will put it all behind me. No? Maybe if I talk it out with my friend. Still, the feelings persisted. Well, then what do I do Lord? In the stillness of my quiet time, when my heart was finally quiet enough to listen, the Lord washed my heart with a question. "Terry," He said sweetly, "which of your sins have I not forgiven?" The answer to my anguish had finally come. It changed my whole perspective. Matthew 6 vs 14-15 says "*For if you forgive other people when they sin against you, your heavenly Father will also forgive you. 15 But if you do not forgive others their sins, your Father will not forgive your sins.*"

So, for me, it was that simple. I had to pardon my Mom's sins towards me just as Christ had pardoned my sins towards Him. So, after praying, I approached my Mother. "Mother, may I?" I asked intently. "May you what?" she replied. "May I help you with anything?" This was my way of surrendering unforgiveness and taking up Christ's forgiveness.

Prayer: Lord, thank You that you forgive me. Allow me to see those around me as you see them. Lord as I battle unforgiveness, I am aware that this is not of You. Empower through Your Spirit to forgive those who do wrong against me. Lord, it is for Your Kingdom and Your glory that we ask it in Jesus Name.

Terry-Ann Talbert

Awakened in Christ

"He that dwelleth in the secret place of the Most High shall abide under the shadow of the Almighty," Psalm 91:1

Being aware and keen to the presence of God is necessary as we attempt to do this thing we identify as "life." When we become awakened that God's presence is with us and we acknowledge this reality our lives can be made new. Never be afraid to begin again. Remember the scriptures are real and edifying.

I remember experiencing my husband having five heart attacks within seven months. Living through this was one of the scariest times of my life. During his fifth heart attack, I was unable to accompany him into the hospital due to COVID-19. Seeing the paramedics wheel my husband in the hospital without me, felt like the very air I breathed was being stunted by the fear that gripped my soul, wondering, will he make it? Oh, but we serve a MIGHTY God!!! As quickly as fear gripped my soul was as quickly as the Holy Spirit reminded me that I dwell in HIS secret place and Kevin would survive this. Continuing in Psalm 91:15-16 I was reminded that, "*He shall call upon me, and I will answer him: I will be with him in trouble; I will deliver him and honor him. With long life will I satisfy him and shew him my salvation."*

This provides guidance on the importance of being awakened in Christ and dwelling with Him daily. It is important that we spend time with the Most High dwelling in His presence on a daily basis. Understanding His predestined will for our lives and coming to the knowledge of this awakening, is an amazing place to begin.

Most Gracious and Almighty God help me to always be mindful of beginning each day as a new awakening and dwelling in your presence. Thank You for the opportunity to come to Your throne of mercy and learn more of You. Help me to never forget to begin each day with You so I will be equipped to face what You have for me. Thank You for remembering Your mercies are new every day! In Yeshua/Jesus Name. Amen!

Dr. Elaine Barclay

God is my Refuge and Strength

"God is within her; she will not fall" Psalm 46:5

I was pregnant with my second child, Laila. My husband and I were so excited to be having a baby girl. Throughout my pregnancy, I stayed vigilant at going to all my doctor's appointments. In my second trimester my OB/GYN told me I would need to see a prenatal specialist because my baby showed on the ultrasound that she was missing some parts of her brain. I was a nervous wreck, crying on and off, not knowing if my baby will be ok. I continued to follow-up multiple times and we had to do genetic counseling to ensure we had no family history of any genetic disorders. I also had to complete an MRI for the specialist to get a closer look at her brain.

Waiting on the results was the hardest thing because as a nurse, you always think the worst possible scenario. I would call my Mom all the time, crying because I wasn't sure what the outcome would be, and she always prayed for my family and told me to pray and stay strong. Then I received the results and the radiologist said, "Every part of her brain is there." We were ecstatic that everything was normal on the MRI. At my follow-up visits, the ultrasound tech asked me if I was sure everything was seen on MRI because on her ultrasound, she was still unable to see a part of her brain. I said, "everything is there, and God is able" and nothing else needed to be said. I am happy to say we had a healthy bouncing 7lb 3 oz baby girl on Valentine's Day! She is a great little sister to her brother, Devon.

God intervened in my situation and I am so grateful. God is my Rock and Shield and a very present help in trouble. He comes through for me no matter what challenges I experience in my life. I desire to continue to trust the Lord my God with all my heart and all my might. No matter how bleak your situation may seem, trust in God. He will always intervene.

Eternal Father, I thank You for always being there when I face challenges in my life. I worship You and magnify Your name. Thank you for Your renewed mercies every day and Your constant love. Keep me in Your love and Your grace. Empower me to do Your will in Jesus' name, Amen!

Nekeisha Basko

Still Standing in His Presence

For day and night, thy hand was heavy upon me; my moisture is turned into the drought of summer. (Psalms 32: 4)

After this prayer, the Psalmist confessed, acknowledged his sin, and submitted himself in God's Hands. God did not prevent His mercy and blessing from the Psalmist, in Psalms 21:2, he stated that God has given him his heart's desire and He has not withheld the request from his heart.

Oh, how wonderful to know that God's hands are always upon His children, even when they transgressed against Him. When the Psalmist David sinned against God, he asked God for forgiveness by completely submitting himself to Him. He cried out to the Lord not only for forgiveness but, for a change of heart and for God to open his eyes. David also called the Lord his hiding place Who preserves him from trouble and who will, in turn, compass him with songs of deliverance. The Psalmist also asked the Lord to teach him in His ways and fill the emptiness in his heart with joy and gladness.

When we sin, we cry out to Him. He is ready to deliver us because of His Love for us. In 1 Peter 2:24-25, God reminded us how He bore our sins on His body on the tree, that we who are dead in sins should live into righteousness.

Like the Psalmist, I acknowledge my sins and submit myself to God so He can work on me. I am aware that it is a daily struggle, but I know I can be victorious with my Lord. I am reminded that when I put my trust in the Lord, He will never leave me nor forsake me.

Dear Jesus, thank You for carrying our sins on the cross. Let Your light shine through us. We honor You! Your glory is great toward us, You deliver us when we call on You. You purify our minds and thoughts because we trust in your deliverance. Guide our hearts to desire the pleasure from Your hands and allow us to dwell in your path until we see You in glory. Amen!

Dr. Maryse Desir

The Faithfulness of God

On January 20, 2014, my husband and I were blessed with our beautiful daughter, Madison Rose Johnson. A few days after the birth of our daughter, I noticed that my legs were swollen and full of edema, and I could barely walk. I thought the swelling of extremities happen during the end of pregnancy not after, especially, since I didn't experience any swelling during my pregnancy.

I was in so much pain, that my family took me to the emergency room, where I was transferred to the ICU. I received numerous antibiotics, pain medications, and units of blood to keep me stable and determine my diagnosis. A few days later, I was diagnosed with an aggressive bacterium that was killing my tissues. It was so aggressive that the bacteria went down my leg all the way up to my stomach wall. The doctors stated that I would need surgery as this was a life-or-death situation. I had to have six surgeries to remove all the dead tissues.

While I was in the hospital, I cried every day. I was unable to see my daughter that I had just given birth to. I couldn't hold her, touch her, or even see her. Throughout my whole ordeal, I had my family and friends praying for me far and near. They had prayer groups and phone calls, praying for God to heal me physically, mentally, and spiritually. Without God and the support of my loving family and friends, I don't know if I would be here to share my story. I continued to pray for the Lord to give me a spirit of crazy faith and the ability to trust in Him no matter what I experience.

Through everything that I've been through, I give thanks. I may not understand some of the events and circumstances that I faced and continue to face in life, but my faith is strong, and I trust in God!!!

Trust in the Lord with all your heart and lean not on your own understanding; in all your ways submit to Him, and He will make your paths straight. - Proverbs 3:5-6

Dear Jesus, thank You for showing up in my situations. You are the Great Physician, You took over from the surgeons, doctors, nurses, and everyone on the medical team and saved my life. I feel Your abiding presence in my life as I submit to You daily. Continue to mold and fashion me in Your likeness and grant me a double portion of Your blessings as I grow in Your grace. In Jesus name Amen!

Kameisha Johnson

A Leap of Faith

"I can do all this through him who gives me strength."
Philippians 4:13

On June 7, 2016, I jumped headfirst into real estate. Not knowing what was ahead, I placed all my faith in God, trust in my vision and my work ethic, knowing this was a new journey that I was embarking on. I went from a salaried employee to now an entrepreneur. Although it sounded quite easy, the road ahead was daunting, to say the least. I had just quit my teaching job and made a vow to myself that I wanted to explore more in life, little did I know that exactly six months later, I was behind on my mortgage, my car note, had a negative bank account, and barely had enough food in the fridge to live. I remember having only $10 on me, sitting in the parking lot going back and forth in my head. I was trying to decide if I should use it to put gas in my car for a showing or spend it on eating dinner that day. I would work long days and nights for months and end up with no leads, no transactions, no contracts, and nothing to show for it.

At my lowest point, I felt as if nothing was going right. I questioned if I made the right decision. I even cried at night praying and asking God what I am doing wrong, and why this was happening to me. I learned more about myself, my mindset, my strengths, and my weaknesses all within a matter of a few months. All the failures, the no's, and the countless disappointments were molding and preparing me to become the woman that I am today. I can tell you my God works in mysterious ways. I couldn't get through my blessing without going through a test!! My mental and spiritual growth changed dramatically.

Three years later, I can proudly say that I am now the team lead of the Home Value Group and director of the Luxury Division at Keller Williams. When I say my God is working for me, I truly mean it!!! I am a living testimony of what faith, hard work, and determination look like. I humbly and graciously thank God for all my successes. I thank him for the worst days of my life as well as the best days. I know that it's only through him that I was able to get through those challenges that shaped me into who I am today. Believe me, when I say God has a plan for every one of us. He has everything all written out for us, we just must trust Him and believe!

"Truly I tell you, if you have faith as small as a mustard seed, you can say to this mountain, 'Move from here to there,' and it will move. Nothing will be impossible for you." Matthew 17:20

Eternal Father, thank You for standing in the gap for me. I give You all the praise and all the glory for being my Rock and Shield

through some of the most difficult times. I desire to continue to grow in Your grace. Please continue to mold me into the person I ought to be. In Jesus name. Amen!

Chante Barrett

Baptize with The Holy Spirit

"I indeed baptize you with water; but One mightier than I is coming, whose sandal strap I am not worthy to loose. He will baptize you with the Holy Spirit and fire." (Luke 3:16, NKJV).

John preached in the wilderness and encouraged the people to be baptized. Many people were baptized in the Jordon River. John explained to the people that he baptized with water, but there is One who is mightier than he who will baptize with the Holy Spirit.

The Holy Spirit was presented to us when Jesus returned to Heaven. The Holy Spirit is our comforter. It speaks to us in accordance with God's words. When we are baptized with the Holy Spirit, we are renewed in the presence of God. We are emptied of self and all the distractions around us, and we are filled with all the attributes of God.

The Holy Spirit brings unspeakable joy and enables us to see points of light in this dark world. Without the Holy Spirit, I would be lost, everything would be chaotic, and there would be no hope. Genesis 1:2 makes it clear, that out of the chaos, the

Holy Spirit hovered over and brought incredible beauty and order.

Is your life seemingly out of control? Would you like to place things in order? Do you want to experience joy in your life? Are you ready for the infilling of the Holy Spirit?

The Holy Spirit is ready to illuminate your life with the love of Jesus. Reach out and accept the Holy Spirit and enjoy a new life in Christ.

I am blessed beyond measure by the power of the Holy Spirit in my life. The Holy Spirit fills me with divine love. He is a gentle friend and a blessed comforter. Although I cannot acclaim that I am a perfect example of everything I have written, I know it is by God's ever-present help and guidance that I strive to become more like Him.

Baptize me anew with Your Holy Spirit. Remove anything that is unlike You and help me to become a vessel that can be used only for Your glory. Wash me in Your Blood and lead me into Your path of righteousness. I ask to "hover o' er me, Holy Spirit" and give me joy, hope, and a new beginning. In Jesus Amen!

Dr. Donna Barrett

Trusting In God

"In God, I will praise His word, in God I have put my trust; I will not fear what flesh can do unto me." Psalms 56:4

We put our trust in people or things that can fail and let us down. But real trust comes from God who is in control of everything and every situation. For us to trust God, we need to have a relationship with Him. Our relationship with God cements our trust in Him. God will take us through any situation we are going through. We can trust that He will never let us down.

In February 2019, I had no idea what I was stepping into when I entered the room. My boss and the HR representative sat on the other side of the table. The news hit hard "We have to let you go because of financial difficulties." Within the next two weeks, I was out of a job. I had college courses I needed to complete and bills to pay. My husband's income would be the only one coming in. I wondered how we would manage. He did not seem worried about it. 'Let's pray about it' he said. We prayed every day and asked God to help us to trust him more. Within this time, I was able to complete my courses. We never ran out of food and our bills were paid every month. We put our trust in God and he provided for us all that we needed.

After several months of being out of a job, God provided a job for me in September 2019. He is an on-time God, He is Awesome and worthy to be praised! Psalms 28:7 says, "The LORD is my strength and my shield; my heart trusted in him, and I am helped: therefore, my heart greatly rejoiceth; and with my song will I praise him." Trust in God and leave everything to Him. Never doubt him for He will provide everything you need and more.

Dear Heavenly Father, I thank You for being there for me and showing up when I needed You the most. Thank You, Father, for providing for me and my family. Almighty God, You are awesome. Help me to always trust You and never doubt that You can fix any and every situation. Help me to give my all to You. In Jesus' name. Amen!

Georgia Alvaranga

Healed of Breast Cancer

In January 2008, I was diagnosed with stage four amino carcinoma breast cancer. One of the most aggressive types of breast cancer. I had no health insurance; however, God opened a way for me to be approved for health insurance twenty-four hours after being diagnosed. My first visit with the oncologist confirmed that I have stage 4 breast cancer. He gave me a treatment plan for ten chemotherapy treatments and sixteen radiation therapy treatments. While undergoing four out of the ten chemotherapy treatments I was very sick, so sick to the point that I lost my hair, eyebrows, and eyelashes. My family and I decided to stop my chemotherapy treatment and seek out alternative holistic care.

I knew that my life was not over, it was just the beginning because I am a believer in God. I began to speak faith words. I spoke healing Scriptures over my life every-day. The good fight of faith became real to me making me want to seek God earnestly. I repented of all my sins and forgave everyone that had done me wrong. God became my obsession, healer, deliverer, provider, lawyer, miracle worker, doctor, light in the darkness I could go on and on. He never stopped working for me. Even when I couldn't see or feel, I kept my faith strong in Him. I am totally healed of cancer and I am twelve years cancer-free.

Isaiah 65:24 "Even before they call, I will answer, and while they're still speaking, I still answer." The Word of God became my daily bread and through it all I allowed all my requests to be made known unto Him. The God of peace shall be my strength. I have learned to praise and worship. I overcame by the blood of the lamb and by the word of my testimony. Faith must work by love. Faith is the root towards what you need to have in order to work on yourself. Faith is what you cannot see but believe. *"Faith is the substance of things hoped for, and the evidence of things not seen." Hebrews 11:1.* Faith is being obedient of God's word. Faith is the main ingredient to begin a relationship with God's words (Mark 11:23).

"Whosoever shall say unto this mountain be thou removed and be cast into the sea and shall not doubt in his heart but shall believe that those things which he saith shall come to pass, he shall have whatsoever he saith." 3 John 1:2. "Beloved I pray above all things that thou mayest prosper and in good health." (Psalms 103:1). The Lord is compassionate and gracious, slow to anger, and abounding in love. Faith is the second aspect of conversion to repentance of sin. Faith is the confidence and trust in God's words. Many of us have had afflictions, but the Lord delivered us.

I can tell you that everything you pray and ask for, believe that you have received it and you shall have it. Elijah was a man subject to passion as we are, and he prayed earnestly for the rain. It didn't rain on the earth for three years and six months. He prayed again, and the heavens gave rain, and the earth brought forth fruit. Another example is the centurion servant. Jesus entered Capernaum, and the people came unto him, saying "Lord my servant is lying at home sick at a point to death". Jesus answered him "I'll come and heal him". The centurions answered, “Lord, I'm not worthy enough that you could come under my roof." The Lord answered him "Speak the word only and your servant shall be healed.

That is what I believe and did. One year after diagnosis God healed my body of cancer. Won't he do it for you!

Dear Jesus thank You for Your healing power. My faith is restored in You. You are my Rock and my Shield and a very present help in the time of trouble. Continue to mold me into the person You want me to be. In Jesus name Amen!

Yvonne Black

Praying for Loved Ones

Therefore, I exhort first of all that supplications, prayers, intercessions, and giving of thanks be made for all men.
1Timothy 2:1

At the tender age of two, I went to live with my grandparents, and as much as I can remember about that age, I was happy. I remember going to church with the neighbors and reciting memory verses, singing in the children's choir, and reciting poems. My grandmother would attend church occasionally to see me perform, and soon we both gave our hearts to the Lord and were baptized.

This started a new atmosphere in the home. My grandmother started praying, especially for my grandfather. It seemed like she would pray for him every day to give his heart to the Lord. I also heard her praying for her siblings, her only daughter (my mom), and her grandchildren; she prayed for the people in the church; she prayed for the neighbors; I began to wonder if she wasn't getting tired of praying for all these people all the time, especially my grandfather. After about 10 years, I cried one day when I saw my grandfather gave his heart to the Lord and got baptized. This is when I learned that God really hears and answers our prayers. When I became a spiritually mature adult, then it was at that time that I understood what my grandma was engaged in. I was called Intercessory prayer. She was praying for God to work on the hearts of the people she cared about.

I now have my own list of people who I pray for continually. I am doing my own intercessory prayers. One of the most beautiful answers to my prayers was the day when one of my sisters called and told me that she had given her life to the Lord and was getting baptized that same day. What a rewarding feeling that was! Jesus prayed for his disciples, and he admonishes us to pray for one another. Jesus himself prayed for us when He was on earth and He is even now interceding for us in the heavenly sanctuary. Wouldn't you make your own prayer list and begin praying for your loved ones? It will be a blessing to see some of your prayers answered in your lifetime. Someone is interceding for you, so why not intercede for someone else? It is never too late to do the right thing. So, go ahead, make that list, and begin praying.

Thank You, Jesus, for praying for me. Give me a heart like Yours so that I will have a desire to pray for others. Amen

Sharon Roberts

Faith

"But when you ask, you must believe and not doubt, because the one who doubts is like a wave of the sea blown and tossed by the wind." James 1:6, NIV

It was September 2016 that I received the diagnosis that no parent ever wants to hear. My two-year-old daughter had bilateral retinoblastoma (cancer of the eye), a life-threatening disease that was not treatable in my homeland. My whole world was turned upside down. The ophthalmologist instructed me to take clothing for my daughter and me for a four-day stay in the hospital. I later discovered that my daughter was scheduled to remove her eyes.

"Do you know of anywhere I could get treatment for her?" I asked, tears streaming down my cheeks. The response was no. I then asked," How long do I have to make a decision before the cancer will start to spread?" He reminded me how aggressive that type of cancer was and gave me three weeks to return for the surgery if I was unsuccessful in finding somewhere to treat her. I had no money, but by faith, I started searching for hospitals overseas in order to get the treatment she needed.

God promised in 1John 5:14 that if we ask anything according to His will, He hears us. Some of my friends came to visit. We prayed and I left the hospital with renewed faith that God will make a way. During the weeks that followed, I was in constant prayer, pleading with God on her behalf and claiming God's promises. My God answered my prayer.

In October 2016, my daughter started her treatment at St. Jude Children's Research Hospital in Memphis. The doctors there worked hard to restore her to good health. She lost an eye, but her life was saved. I did not receive a bill for treatment; God had indeed made a way. Today, she is a happy six-year-old who graduated as the valedictorian of her kindergarten class.

It was not an easy journey, but sometimes God must take us out of our comfort zone for us to realize that we should trust him. Step out in faith, trust the Lord to do the impossible things in your life. He has promised never to leave us nor forsake us. God loves us with an everlasting love, and he will take care of us.

Heavenly Father, oftentimes we worry because we tend to forget that You have promised in Your words to take care of us. Help us to remember that when we pray and ask for help, we should not doubt, but have confidence in You, knowing You are always there for us.

Sonia Black

Forgiveness

"To whom we have redemption through his blood, the forgiveness of sins, according to the riches of his grace." Eph. 1:7

Forgiveness is the ability to give up and put aside any feelings of ill will or resentment against someone who has deliberately caused you harm. Forgiveness allows you to move on in life without hindrance from the negative feelings of resentment which can stymie your physical, mental, and spiritual growth. The root word of forgiveness is "Perdonare" a Latin word from which we derive The English word "Pardon." Mark Twain wrote "Forgiveness is the fragrance that the violet sheds on the heel that has crushed it. It's one of the greatest gifts you can give yourself is to forgive."

I have as a child and now a woman heard people repeatedly say, "It's hard to forgive someone who has done you wrong and caused serious harm to you." Or "I will forgive but I won't forget." I must confess I am guilty of having used those same words too. However, when I think of the plan of salvation, how Jesus sacrificed his life at Calvary to save humanity from sin, to give mankind an opportunity to choose life over death without harboring any ill will, I know I have fallen short by my words and actions which is not reflective of the spirit of Christ. As a believer in God's word and as an individual who is trying my best to diligently practice the word, I should be able to forgive without reservation if I want to enter the kingdom of heaven.

Peter, the disciple asked God the question "Lord how oft shall my brother sin against me and I forgive him? Till seven times." to which Jesus responded, "I say not unto thee until seven times but, until seventy times seven." In God's plan of salvation, his love for mankind was and is exhibited by his death on the cross for which we can never repay. His unselfish act is priceless, for without the shedding of blood there would be no remission of sin for mankind. His mercy and grace sustained us, for where sin abounded, grace did much more abound. In my weak mortal human state, I have pled with God to help me to transform this part of my character, by yielding my will to His will and practicing the fruits of the spirit of which forgiveness is one of them.

Dear kind and heavenly loving Father help me to forgive others as You have forgiven me. I also realize that I must be able to forgive myself by not holding onto my regrets over life or over things that I simply can no longer change. Give me the power to embrace Your love, salvation open to a desire for me to be saved in Your kingdom. Thank You, Lord, for hearing my prayer, making whole, and for saving my sin-sick soul.

Faith D. Housen

God's Amazing Grace

But grow in grace, and in the knowledge of our Lord and Savior Jesus Christ. To Him be glory both now and forever. Amen.

I was taking care of my mother, who was bedridden while raising two young children (8 and 7 years respectively), as well as working outside of the home. The last of a series of caregivers left without giving me notice and I decided not to hire another.

At that time, I lived in the North-Eastern area of my country and worked as an afternoon shift Teacher (12:30-5:15 pm) at a school in the South-Central District (not close to home), I took public transportation as I did not drive then. As a new school was built very close to where I lived, I requested a transfer to that school. At the Ministry of Education, I was told that in order to receive a transfer, I needed to find someone to replace me.

Even though that was strange, I found someone whom I took to the Ministry of Education, but the person was sent to a different school. I was both bewildered and disappointed. Then my mother died. Two weeks later, a Teacher reported to my

Principal saying that he was sent there as a replacement. *He was there to replace me.* You see, at the new school close to my home, the day started at 7:55 am. God knew that it would be difficult for me to take care of my Mother, get the children off to school, and be on time for 7:55. So, in His grace, He worked it out the way He did.

God works in mysterious ways. His timing is always right and may be quite different from ours. That is the lesson that I learned from that experience.

Dear God, I pray for all the women who are facing challenging circumstances. May they develop a strong faith, knowing that, at the right time, You will send relief because you are interested in every detail of their lives; and that they are living under Your grace.

Brenda Ferdinand

No Favoritism

"My brothers, as believers in the Lord Jesus Christ, don't show favoritism. But if you show favoritism, you sin and are convicted by the law as lawbreakers." (James 2:1, 9 NIV)

"Everything was great until mom had a new baby," 16 years old Sabrina began, as she told the story of her painful childhood.

A major hurricane hit the small island on which we lived. My real mother's home was blown away by the storm. My siblings and I were forced to find shelter at the neighbor's house. It felt safe there. After three days, my two sisters and one brother went with our mother to some unknown place. In my childhood innocence, I begged to stay with the family that would later adopt me as their daughter. Mom was kind. She provided me with lots of pretty clothes, toys, good food, and fun. Dad was my best friend. As their only child, I went everywhere they went and was treated royally.

Shortly before my sixth birthday, Mom had a new baby. He was cute and I was happy to have a brother. However, I began to feel jealous. He was getting all of Mom's love. I cried often because I felt neglected. That made my mom angry. So, she began to beat on me, and she spoke to me harshly, most of the time. At age ten, I ran away from home. Then, I found comfort in telling lies, bullying other children at school and I was generally the teacher's nightmare.

My dad tried to be my best friend, at least when we were not around my mother. She cursed at him and spoke evil of the two of us, many times. Within 8 years, I had 3 siblings. As we grew up things got worse. I became everybody's servant. I was as hurt emotionally as I was physically abused. To put an end to it, I left home and never contacted my parents for over a year. However, I called my siblings occasionally. It was a privilege to take this young lady under my care and to keep calling to God for help (Psalm 18:6) on her behalf. She has recovered from her depressed, angry state and even forgave her mom for being so mean. I am glad that she did because her mom died soon after.

In God's sight, everyone is equal and deserves to be loved without condition. Let's intercede for parents behaving badly toward their adopted children and showing favoritism between them and their biological children. That is unacceptable behavior.

Dear Lord, thank You for the privilege to share my family with others who are victims of social abuse. Kindly provide warmth and inclusion for those who are not loved by their own families. Do bring restoration to such families and let them know that You care.

His Purpose for My Life

He who did not spare His own Son, but delivered Him up for us all, how shall He not with Him also freely give us all things?
Romans 8:32, NKJV

Have you ever wondered what is God's purpose for your life? If so, you are not alone. I and countless others have wondered the same. Christians and those who don't profess faith in God, alike, have grappled with this question. The question concerning the purpose of life is one of what I like to call life's three big questions: Where did I come from? What is my purpose for being here? Where am I going or Is there something to hope for after death?

What we think about our life's purpose has much to do with our beliefs about our origin. Were we created by a loving Being who had a purpose for our lives, did we come into existence through random processes that evolved over billions of years, or did an angry and jealous being create us through a violent process as the historical epics of some cultures depict? I choose to believe that I was created by a loving God who, not only created me in

His image but sent His Son to redeem me after sin entered the earth and marred His image in human beings. I choose to believe that such a loving God that would leave the splendor of His heavenly abode and the worship and adoration of the angelic hosts to be spat upon and crucified by the ones He came to save must have a purpose for my life. After all, who would create beings in His image, die for them, and express unconditional love and unimaginable patience with them if He had no purpose for them? With most humans, after three offensive strikes, we are likely to sever ties with those who offend us. Imagine a God who has borne patiently and graciously with us for several thousand years! Would that God not have a purpose for my life? Would that God not have a purpose for your life? I believe He does.

There are times when I become uncertain about the purpose of life in the sense of what career path I should take, where I should live, whom I should marry, and such like. Whenever such thoughts try to dominate, the Bible points me back to the main purposes for my life, to glorify God, to love others as God loves me, and to share the good news of His salvation and Second Coming. These three purposes help me to regain my focus, remind me to make seeking God's kingdom and His righteousness the number one priority of my life, and that God will take care of the temporal issues if I put Him first. *Matthew 6:33* So far, I have not found better purposes for my life than those found in His Word. And you know what? I never will! God's road maps for each of His children may look slightly different, but they will always be based on those three foundational purposes. What is clouding your spiritual vision today and causing you to question God's purpose for your life? Remember that the One who brought you into existence and redeemed you *must and does* have a purpose for you. Trust Him!

Dear God, help me to realize the main purposes for which you created me: to glorify You, to love others as You love me, and to share the good news of Your Salvation and Second Coming. Help me to give You first place in my life and trust You to meet my temporal needs, in Jesus' name and for His sake, I pray. Amen!

Susan Gay

Trusting in God

What time I'm afraid, I will trust in thee. Psalm 57:3

Life is always throwing challenges at us which sometimes causes us to be afraid. If we believe the word of God, we should not be afraid. Psalm 91:5 says "Thou shalt not be afraid for the terror by night; nor for the arrow that flieth by day." Battles are won when we trust in God's power.

In 1987 when it was time for me to migrate to the United States of America, I was unprepared. My passport was not ready because I thought I had a longer time to get it done. I was given a short time to report to the embassy with my passport which I thought was impossible. However, I decided to trust God, I went to the passport office to make an application and the crowd was unbelievable I sat down thinking there was no hope. To my surprise I saw a man looking at me then he called me with his fingers, wondering what his reason for was calling me. I walked over to him. Then he said to me "do you remember me?" I replied, "no sir," he said "don't you remember Dwight"

I started brainstorming but came up with no remembrance of him he said to me I am one of your past students from your youth Sabbath school class at the New Haven Seventh-day Adventist Church. That's when I remembered who he was and fortunately, he was the supervisor. He said, "how can I help you" and I said, "I needed a passport in two weeks" I was given some papers to be filled out and returned to him at a certain date. Then I was given another date to come back to see him surprisingly when I went back, I was handed my passport. My conclusion is when we trust in the Lord, He will supply all our needs.

Lord, I thank You for who You are. I can trust You now and always. Thank You for your grace and mercy In Jesus' Name Amen!

Florence Sinclair

Wait on the Lord

Wait on the Lord be of good courage, and he will strengthen thine heart: wait, I say, on the Lord. Psalm 27:14

Years ago, after I finished teacher's college it was very difficult to find a job. I must have sent out what felt like hundreds of resumes with no response. It was a very frustrating time especially since funds were low during that time. I prayed and prayed, and nothing happened. I continued to send out resume after resume, still nothing. It was now August, and the start of school was in September and I was beginning to lose faith that I will get a job by then.

One day while browsing a teacher's website I saw my dream job and they were looking for a teacher with my "teachable" (subjects I am qualified to teach). I quickly applied for the job and in the meantime, I waited and waited with no response. It wasn't until the last week of August that I received a phone call from the school asking me to come in for an interview. I was beside myself with excitement, so I prayed again, thanking God for the interview and I claimed this job in Jesus' name. I did the interview and was told a day later that I did not get the job because they found someone who was more experienced than me. I was upset and began to question God. "Lord, did you not say we should ask, and we will receive?" I was feeling frustrated again. But in the waiting period, He reminded me to sit still, shut up, and watch Him work.

This was now the middle of September and still nothing. A few days later I received a phone call saying this same school would like to add me to their supply list, and even better, by October, the position was available. I was reminded of God's promise to wait on Him and to be of good courage. Through all of this, I learned patience, perseverance, and that God is indeed a promise keeper.

Father God, you are wonderful and awesome! Thank You for the lessons on waiting and the reminder that everything You do is for our best interest, which is motivated by Your love for us. Amen!

Ann Marie Troupe-Afflick

Serving God Through Serving Others

"Now is God so clothes the grass of the field, which today is, and tomorrow is thrown into the oven, will He not much more clothe you, O you of little faith?" Matthew 6: 30

The Sabbath morning started off better considering the week I had. I was trying not to worry about all the things I wanted to get but couldn't because there was no money to do so. Coming to church and not having to worry about all that but the things of life made a difference. Seeing my mother and my church family receiving hugs and kisses and well wishes was a breath of fresh air. My mother then handed me an envelope from my sister in West Palm. After I got to my seat, I opened it, only to find a crisp $100. My friend and I started giving praises. Not even five minutes later it was caring and sharing time. As a sister went up to the front of the church, already I had a foreboding feeling that it was going to be a big /dramatic announcement.

A family member amongst us was in dire need and might lose her house if she didn't get a specific amount of money before a specified date in the week, she stated. My palms started to get sweaty because I could hear and feel the Holy Spirit impressing me to give the contents of my envelope. But I did what I thought was best for me, I ignored her. Then suddenly, my friend turned to me and said, I know you don't want to hear this, but the Holy Spirit told me to tell you that you should offer up what's in the envelope, I instantly started crying because I too had felt the prompting and although it was hard, I couldn't now deny what I was being asked to do. In life, I always made it an important aim to do what the Lord commands even if it's not always easy. However, this time I needed the money, not direly but I still needed it. Funny thing though after I gave it up, I was at peace and church progressed in a beautiful time in Zion.

At the end of service, one of my church aunts came up to me and gave me an envelope and to my amazement when I opened it was a $100 bill. God had given me the money back and on the same day. Talk about timing. That day I truly learned that I need to trust God more and when I'm asked to be His hand here on earth. I have no need to worry because God is our provider. Even before we ask, He had already made the way for provision. I'm not going to lie though; I still do struggle with letting go and giving it all to God at times but every time that happens, I'm reminded of the many times God has taken me through hills and valleys. I've asked in the past and He has always provided. Indeed, I can rest assured knowing that God has already and will always provide.

Dear Lord, thank You for being Jehovah Jireh my provider, thank You for Your promise that even before I ask You will answer. May I learn that when we serve others, we grow in serving You. Amen!

Kaye Ann Clarke

God's Amazing Grace

"And he said unto me, My grace is sufficient for thee: for my strength is made perfect in weakness, most gladly, therefore, will I rather glory in my infirmities, that the power of Christ may rest upon me." 2 Cor. 12:9

Why am I here? But for God's amazing grace. I don't deserve God's love, again but for His amazing grace. My transformed life is a definite testimony to what He will do for you through His wonderful, amazing grace and power. His amazing matchless saving grace is obtained when you grasp His hands with a willing submissive spirit and allow Him to lead and guide you through life's unchartered changing pathway.

God is unique. There is none like Him. His compassion and grace toward humanity are unmatched. Everything He created on this earth was done in love for the benefit of mankind, even though He knew mankind would reject Him repeatedly. In His omniscient power, He prepared the plan of salvation ahead of time, to rescue fallen man. He sacrificed himself through shedding His blood on Calvary's tree for the remission of mankind's sin. He displayed loyalty, mercy, and grace to an undeserving human race. His heart was broken due to the rejection of His kind tender love. He did not retaliate in anger, but with much tender care and love, wooed us back to Him with open arms; readily and willingly waiting for those who would accept Him. God knew that where sin abounded His grace would much more abound.

God's amazing grace is seen on full display in the lives of the children of Israel during the period of the Exodus, under the leadership of Moses. The children of Israel were rebellious and ungrateful. They quickly forgot every trial that God had successfully brought them through. They forgot how God rescued them and supplied their physical and spiritual needs. Instead, they murmured and complained, they longed to return to Egypt as slaves, in order to practice idolatry, riotous, and a demoralizing living. God was patient, He became angry, but Moses pleaded with Him. Love shone through. God's mercy and amazing grace sprang into action. He forgave them, wiped the slate clean, and started all over again. God knew of mankind's natural propensity towards sin. It is the reason why He became sin, who knew no sin for us to deliver us from a fallen world.

The profound impact on the lives of mankind transformed by God's amazing grace is remarkable. The impact may vary in degrees but once delivered from sin the recipient has something to sing, shout, smile, and cry about in sincerest appreciation of what God has done for him. He becomes a witness to the world that God's amazing grace is real and is available for anyone who comes to Him in deep contrition.

Dear Lord and Father of mankind forgive our foolish ways. Your Amazing grace has brought us this far and it will continue to lead us home. It will give us the strength to face each new day from a different perspective with a heart full of gratitude. Thank you, Lord, Amen!

Faith D. Housen

Intercessory Prayer – In the Hands of My Father

"Praying at all times in the Spirit, with all prayer and supplication. To that end, keep alert with all perseverance, making supplication for all the saints," Ephesians 6:18 ESV

One day after work I got a phone call from my father.

"Hey, Chrissy."

"Hey Daddy ", I replied. "What's going on?"

I was not ready for what my father was about to tell me. He had prostate cancer and that he would be going into surgery the following month. I can't remember what either of us said after he said "cancer." I was so stunned. After I hung up is when the tears began to flow, and the anger began to erupt. I couldn't understand why my father, a man who loved God so much, taught his children to do the same, and dedicated his life to serving God and his church, would get cancer.

I left my house, hopped in my car in search of clarity. I ended up at my church. I marched into my pastor's office and plopped myself in one of his chairs. He looked up from his work and waited for me to begin. At the end of my tirade, he reminded me that he had survived not one, but two different cancers.

"All you can do is pray for him and leave him in God's hands." He said to me.

Well, I had no idea how much I would have to leave in God's hands that month as my infant niece was rushed into surgery for an infection and my mother for a torn retina. I prayed, my family prayed, and my church family prayed. Each of them had difficult recoveries. But we were all together for Christmas and doing much better. My mother regained her sight but then later the following year lost it completely. But I still have every one of those family members in my life and I thank God for getting them and my family through such a difficult time.

Lord, thank You for still being willing to hear our prayers even when we're hurt and upset. Thank You for helping those we love in their time of need.

Christine Thompson

His Purpose for my Life

"But I have raised You up for this very purpose, that I might show You my power and that my name might be proclaimed in all the earth." Exodus 9:16, NIV.

I'm almost sure that we have all heard children, or a person being classified as mistakes, whether in person or through the grapevine. You might have even been called one too! I used to ignore the comment, but after getting to know God some more, I have found it harder to bite my tongue, even if it's from a total stranger's lips. Just skimming over scientific data would convince an atheist to correct:

A. Out of billions of sperm cells, it took only one to hit the egg just the right way. It is literally one out of nearly two billion.

B. Even now when it is fertilized, there is only one out of three chances that the egg will develop.

C. About a half of those that do develop, never even make it to implantation in the uterus.

D. Even if it makes the cut, the poor little guy isn't safe just yet. Only three-quarters of pregnancies survive. Eighty-five percent of the lost quarter happens in the first twelve weeks. Sometimes, even before a woman is aware that she might be pregnant.

Let me not even go into the statistics of how many children die during birth or soon after. Every time I hear the phrase, "That child/person was a mistake," I think about Jeremiah when God spoke those beautiful words, "Before I formed thee in the belly, I knew thee, and before thou camest forth out of the womb I sanctified thee, and I ordained thee a prophet unto the nations." *Jeremiah: 1:5, KJV*. Through the pen of inspiration, Cory Asbury of Bethel Music placed one of my favorite songs onto paper, "Reckless Love." He wrote, "Before I took a breath, You breathe Your life into me..." What more do we need to know that God knows what He is doing? In His amazing wisdom, He molded us and commissioned us to do His work, but only if we so desire (He never forces us to be about His business; isn't choice a glorious thing?). Furthermore, He thought of us before our parents could even think to consider our conception.

Out of infinite choices, He chose you and me! We're not here by some random alignment of the galaxy or the sun, moon, and stars, luck or chance. You were chosen! Hand-selected by God Himself. How can we ever see that as anything but Him being His amazing self? How can we ever think that we weren't meant to be here, in this place, for such a time as this? Even if you don't believe it, I know that my God never makes mistakes; you aren't one!

Dear All-Knowing God, I pray that when we feel inadequate or like we are mistakes, we remember the care You placed into us even being conceived. Help us to remember that it is not by accident that we are here. In Your infinite wisdom, You have fashioned us into beings to glorify You. Let us then never deliberately bring shame to Your name or character. In Your Son's name, I pray. Amen.

"And we know that in all things God works for the good of those who love Him, who have been called according to his purpose." Romans 8:28, NIV.

Alexandira Espeut-Thompson

Overcome Evil with Good

"Therefore, if thine enemy hunger, feed him; if he thirsts, give him drink: for in so doing, thou shalt heap coals of fire on his head. Be not overcome of evil but overcome evil with good."
Romans 12:20, 21

I have always admired David praying about his enemies in the book of Psalms, especially when he spared the life of Saul on two occasions. I wonder what I would have done if that was me. Then in the New Testament Jesus tells us to do good to our enemies and pray for them. However, we can never fully understand what that means until we have an experience of our own.

This was not the usual Monday morning. I did not want to go to that place, work. I was recently informed that one of my coworkers was making accusations about me. Everyone knew that it was false and wanted me to take revenge. They could not understand how I was still being so kind to her when I was aware of what she was doing. My answer was the same every time. If I say that I am a Christian, then I can't do otherwise.

I made this situation a subject of prayer. My husband prayed. I asked for prayer at the Wednesday night prayer meeting at church. I continued to be kind and was encouraged by another sister when she reminded me of today's text in one of her devotions.

Fast forward six weeks. Problems arose on the job, which called for the Supervisor's investigation. That Wednesday was my day-off and I was quite happy to be home and relaxed in peace and quiet. As I got to work on Thursday morning, I was greeted with the words, "did you hear?" "Hear what?" I replied. I was then informed that my coworker got fired on Wednesday while I was at home. I felt sad. Those looking at me expected me to rejoice but I just kept quiet. As we went to our various stations of work, I started talking to Jesus. I said Lord, I didn't want her to lose her job, I just wanted her to leave me alone. However, if this is how you choose to answer my prayer, please help her to find a job soon. The verse came to me, "Vengeance is mine, I will repay said the Lord."

This payment was very stern in my opinion, but God says we are the apple of His eye and He holds us in the palm of His hand. When we take our problems to Him in prayer, He hears and answers them, but we must be in His will. In this case, today's text was my test. It doesn't matter what your enemies do to you or say to you, let the love of Jesus always shine through.

Dear God, thank You for showing us how to love those who are not so lovable. Thank You for the victory we receive which can only come through You, in Jesus' name. Amen!

Sharon Roberts

God's Amazing Grace-Struggling with Specific Sin

"Come now, and let us reason together," says the* L*ORD*, *"Though your sins are like scarlet, they shall be as white as snow; though they are red like crimson, they shall be as wool. Isaiah 1:18, NKJV

Can Christians struggle with specific sins? Yes, they can. However, struggling to overcome specific sins is different than blatant disregard for the principles of God's Word that govern our lives. Our experience may be like what the apostle Paul described in Romans 7, where we know and want to follow God's principles but find ourselves doing things contrary to what we believe. Our struggle with specific sins is often based on addictions, hereditary traits, life experiences, attempts to fill the voids in our lives, and, even, our reluctance to give up something we cherish, though we know it is harmful.

For years, I struggled with a specific sin, and though I wanted to overcome, I also cherished it. It was a tug-of-war I hated, but I also liked it. I hated it because I knew it was wrong, but I liked it because it gave me comfort and appealed to my pride. I would pray about it and would have periods of victory. In fact, it was these periods of victory that gave me hope that I could completely overcome with God's help. The Holy Spirit also gave me other revelations regarding overcoming. Besides being honest with God and confessing my fondness for the sin, my knowledge that it was wrong, and asking for His help to overcome, I also prayed fervently for Him to take away my desire for it and give me a hatred for it. The Holy Spirit also helped me explore what triggered my desire to engage in this sin and what voids in my life I was attempting to fill.

After months of praying based on these revelations, with some successes and some failures, I got the victory over that specific sin. God answered my earnest and persistent prayers by taking away my desire for the sin, helping me to see it for what it was, and giving me displeasure for it. Another turning point in my struggle came was when I realized that each time I am tempted to sin, I have a choice. Temptation is not a sin; it is when we yield to the temptation that we sin. Though we can deliberately place ourselves in situations where we will be tempted, even then, we have a choice to give in to the temptation or not to yield to it. However, we should try to avoid situations that may tempt us to sin, especially if it is a trigger.

My reason for sharing such a personal experience is to encourage you and for you to encourage others who are struggling with specific sins that are revealed, suspected, or unrevealed. It is through God's goodness and unconditional love that we are led to repentance. *Romans 2:4* Praise be to God who causes us to triumph by giving us the desire and power to overcome! *Philippians 4:13*

Dear God, give me the desire and power to overcome ______ (tell God the specific sin). I don't want anything to come between us that will cause me to separate myself from Your love and be lost eternally. Thank You for loving me so much that you sent Jesus to die for my sins and give me eternal life, in Jesus' name and for His sake, I pray. Amen! – Susan Gay

Your Will Dear Lord, Not Mine

"Saying, Father, if thou be willing, remove this cup from me: nevertheless, not my will, but thine, be done." Luke 22:42

Marianne was known to be a bright girl from a very young age. Around the age of seven, she already decided what she wanted to be in life, and unlike her friends, had no intention of changing her mind. She decided she was to run her own pediatric center being the head doctor of course, and no one else. She chose this profession because growing up, she often found herself at pediatrics with a new problem or diagnosis every time. Just like her doctor was always there for her, she wanted to do the same for little boys and girls who suffered the same plight as her, living an immunocompromised life.

From middle school, she amazed teachers by having most of her life planned out and already knowing what she was aiming for. This continued out throughout high school, college, and medical school as well. Little did Marianne know what Christ had in store for her. Growing up believing in the Seventh Day Adventist belief, she acknowledged that her life wasn't her own and despite all the meticulous planning she had done, Christ could have something else in store for her. Although she acknowledged it, she hoped deep down that her plan would align with His plan and she could live out her dream job. To conclude every prayer she said, "Your will dear Lord, not mine… but please be the same as mine! In Your name, I pray, Amen."

After completing 20 years of education, her plan altered a little in which she desired to be a pediatric surgeon. It was now where Marianne's life was drastically changed. Just as she was about to begin her residency at a top hospital, she felt a calling to go abroad to Southeast Asia to practice not just physical medicine but spiritual medicine as well. She felt the need to use her talents to spread God's word. This meant giving up the lavish lifestyle of a pediatrician in the States, to humble herself and be a beacon and ambassador for Christ in Asia. She knew she could not make the decision on her own, so for the first time in years she prayed *"Your will dear Lord, not mine. In Your name, I pray, Amen."* The following days were a rollercoaster for Marianne in which her mind was decided, but her heart was not. She prayed and fasted with her parents for three days and as soon as the clock struck midnight to end the fast, a voice in her head whispered "Asia." She ran back to her parents and began preparing for the new life she had ahead of her. As a 16-year-old about to embark on her junior year of high school with her whole life planned out, I acknowledge what happened to Marianne can very well happen to me. If that is the case, I pray He will do with me whatever He intends at that my heart will be willing. Her parents acknowledged that she was not mentally prepared for any of it because she planned out a whole new life, so they prayed this prayer with her:

"Dear Lord. Thank You for the plans you have for my life. Although I may want to pursue different things, I pray that You will take my hand and lead me wherever You want me to go. I am Your beacon and Your ambassador. I place all of me and my trust in You. Please hold my hand and lead me in the right direction. If I ever stray from You, please open my eyes to return to You. Lastly, Lord, I pray these words: Your will dear Lord, not mine. In your name, I pray, Amen."

Alyssa Clarke

God Answer Prayers on Time

And we know that all things work together for good to them that love God, to them who are the called according to his purpose.
Romans 8, 28 KJV

Every night before I go to sleep, I ask God to take charge of my life, I repent of my daily mistakes, ask for forgiveness, and thank Him for His many blessing. In the morning, I thank God for another day. I ask Him to reveal the plan He has for my life. My desire is to embrace the purpose He has for me and walk in that purpose. God made each of us in His own unique way, He will reveal our special gift. However, He cannot reveal His will while we still clinging to our own selfish desires. As I reflect on His goodness and mercies, I praise Him and give Him thanks for His blessing despite the ups and downs in my life. God knows exactly what I want before I ask, He will deliver according to His will.

I work in a pediatric cardiologist office for over thirteen and a half years as a medical assistant/administrator. In 2018, there was a turning point where I needed to leave that job. I prayed every day for God to show me a way out. I received the answer one night when I heard a voice telling me to pursue real estate. I registered for the real estate class, attended classes, worked very hard and passed the class exam. As I prepared for the state exam, there was a very big challenge brewing in my personal life. It was a challenging time; however, I went ahead and took the exam. I failed the exam, the first, second, and third time. I was very sad and asked God why I failed the exam three times after I had studied so hard. That night, I heard a still small voice; "don't give up," My faith was restored, and I was determined to pass this exam.

When I thought I was ready, I took the exam again, I failed the exam the fourth, fifth, and sixth time. I became very angry after the sixth attempt and again questioned the Lord. Just as I was about to give up, I went to church for a Wednesday night prayer meeting. I knelt at the altar and prayed earnestly for divine intervention. I got up off my knees and felt total relief from all, my problems. The still small voice echoed in my ear, "take the test, you will pass it the seventh time Seven is a perfect number. I immediately scheduled for the exam. The next few days, I stepped into the testing center with renewed confidence. After I completed the exam, I felt a sense of relief. After a few minutes, the lady smiled and handed my score to me. When I saw "PASS" I shouted Praise the Lord!! I thought about the number seven and what it means; I realized it was God's perfect number; on the seventh day, He sanctified it, the seven candlesticks, the seven churches, and the seventh dip in Jordan river by Naaman.

After the passing of my exam, I asked the Lord to allow me to work my present job until August 2020. This would give me enough time to prepare for a shift to my new career. In February 2020, the coronavirus pandemic took over the entire world. In April 2020, I was furlough for 13 weeks from my job. During this time, I prayed earnestly for the Lord to intervene and open a way. At the end of the furlough, I received a call from the regional manager. She advised me that my position was no longer available, and I will be paid for eight weeks plus all my vacation time. When I hung up the phone, I shouted "Praise the Lord for Your marvelous and matchless grace. We must trust the Lord with everything in our lives for He answer prayers at the right time.

Eternal Father, thank You for answering my prayer at the time I needed it most. Thank You for my life and the way You have carried me through. Help me to stay focus on You and always trust in You, in Jesus' name I pray. Amen!

Carmen Palmer

The Power of Plentiful Potent Prayers

"Is any sick among you? Let him call for the elders of the church; and let them pray over him, anointing him with oil in the name of the Lord." James 5:14

In April of the year two thousand and twenty, I received the devastating news that my dear friend and former colleague in education had been in a terrible car accident. The news was both unimaginable and heart-wrenching. Mere weeks before, she had played a major role in assisting me in sorting out various aspects of my relocation, as I sought to continue with a new teaching appointment in South Florida.

The news was in that she had been seriously injured, was initially unconscious, and had already undergone emergency surgeries. She also had an additional surgery scheduled for later that week. I then sought to do what would have been the only thing I could do, pray, and ask others to pray for her, also.

I began sending messages to all those who I believed I could depend on to say a word on her behalf. Those contacted included family members, friends, church members, pastors, and others, who, though at varied locations, had one common goal, prayer for my friend's healing and recovery. Prayers continued for her as the days rolled by. She was eventually discharged from the hospital and transferred to another facility where she did physical therapy and made great strides. Meanwhile, I continued to update my "prayer team" and we all prayed wherever we were for her swift and successful recovery.

The results of the prayers that were offered on her behalf are nothing short of a miracle. She is indeed a living, breathing example of what prayer can do. The transformation she has experienced from severe injury to swift and successful recovery is a reminder of the breakthrough that we too can experience when others petition God's throne on our behalf.

There are so many things that we can do to demonstrate our care and appreciation for those we love. It would be marvelous to shower them with the gift of prayer today.

Loving Father, I thank You for the gift of prayer. Please show me how to use this gift to be a blessing to others in Jesus' name, Amen.

Beverley Monroe

Hold On

"God is our refuge and strength, a very present help in trouble."
Psalm 46:1

Sometimes we may become so discouraged with the cards that life deals us. Our faith could be tested, and we may begin to wonder if life is worth living. Whatever the depths of despair to which we sink, one thing is certain, if we continue to hold on to God, even when we don't understand, we can trust that He's going to keep us in His care.

Some years ago, my sister was in depression, but people who are suffering from depression are adept at masking their condition, so we did not know what was going on, but God knew. Much later she explained that she knew something was not right. She could not understand why she did not feel right, and couldn't function as she should, so she kept on her knees praying, asking for help. What she didn't realize was that God was trying to show her what was wrong. A voice kept urging her to read a particular magazine, but she was always distracted and didn't. When she finally decided to, the middle article explained depression. It seemed to be describing her life! This made her more convinced that she needed God to help her, and she kept praying. Her life seemed dismal, and at one point she thought that she was no use to herself or society, so she might as well die. The enemy of souls had her considering ending her life and she said that night, God spoke to her. She heard a voice asking, "After all of this, do you want to be lost?" She realized that it was God and cried out to Him to save her! She fell to her knees and woke up the next morning still on her knees.

This was the beginning of a long road to recovery, and in the process of time, God worked with her and healed her. She never saw a doctor or therapist for her condition. God was her refuge and strength, her healer, her help in her time of trouble. As she communed with Him; she developed a closer relationship with Him and found her way back!

I'd like to make it clear that this was her journey. It does not mean that one should not seek professional help when faced with depression. In fact, God may lead someone else to do just that. My sister can't stop praising and thanking God for His grace and mercy, and every opportunity she gets to share His goodness is a joy to her. Whatever the trial, let's not lose heart, but always hold on to God because His Grace and Mercy will keep us no matter what we're going through. He has promised to never leave us or forsake us. I can't imagine how close I came to losing my sister! No matter what, Hold On!

Dear God, thank You for your amazing grace that saves us in known and unknown situations. We cannot go through this life without You, Lord. Help us to always trust in You and hold on to You no matter what trials we face. Amen!

Judith Alexander

Forgiveness

"Therefore, as God's chosen people, holy and dearly loved, clothe yourselves with compassion, kindness, humility, gentleness, and patience. Bear with each other and forgive one another if any of you has a grievance against someone. Forgive as the Lord forgave you" Col. 3:12-13.

After divorcing my husband, I harbored many feelings of anger, hurt, resentment, and unforgiveness towards him because of what had transpired during and after the marriage. For many years I held on to those feelings having convinced myself that I was justified and entitled to do so. I even verbalized on many occasions that I would never forgive him.

As the years passed, and even though the relationship improved immensely, I still held on to the spirit of unforgiveness. I believed that I was justified in withholding "my forgiveness" because he had not done anything to deserve it. I wanted him to come to me and admit that he had wronged me and apologize for his actions and behavior during and after the marriage. In my mind, I was 'owed' this. I made a conscious decision that I would continue to feel this way for the rest of my life. Whilst at the same time acknowledging and accepting that refusing to forgive is violating scripture. Not realizing, that, forgiveness was about me being able to move on from the past and live-in freedom in the present.

My deliverance came on a Palm Sunday morning when there was a guest Evangelist bringing the message. She taught on the concept of forgiveness. As children of God, we need to know that He forgives us and enables us to forgive others and teaches that if we want to experience the freedom that comes from forgiving someone else. We need to experience the forgiveness God wants to introduce into our lives. This message cut me like a double-edged sword. I repented. I was brought to my knees crying out for forgiveness from God for my hardened heart. As a follower of Christ, I totally surrendered. It was at this moment that I felt a heavyweight lifted from my shoulders. I felt a lightness. Like I was floating. My chains of bondage fell away. I felt free!!

One of the things that Nelson Mandela is famous for is his insistence on a policy of forgiveness as opposed to revenge when he became President of South Africa in 1994. In one of His most famous quotes on his release from prison he said, "*As I walked out the door toward the gate that would lead to my freedom, I knew if I didn't leave my bitterness and hatred behind, I'd still be in prison.*"

Forgiveness is for our own growth and happiness. When we hold on to hurt, pain, resentment, and anger it harms us far more than it harms the other person. Forgiveness frees us to live in the present. Our anger, regret, hatred, or resentment towards someone means that we are giving up our power to that person. We are to forgive others (even if we think they do not deserve it) because we were forgiven by God when we did not deserve it. Are you still in chains to the person who has hurt you? Would you like to be free from the bitterness that is binding you and preventing you from moving forward in your life? Take some time right now to admit to God that you have been hurt. Then confess any desires for revenge you may have felt and pray along these lines.

"Lord, I choose to forgive (name of person) for (list what the person did that hurt you) even though it made me feel (painful memories or feelings)

Debra Johnson-King

Stand

"But take heed to yourselves: for they shall deliver you up to councils; and in the synagogues, ye shall be beaten: and ye shall be brought before rulers and kings for my sake, for a testimony against them...But when they shall lead you, and deliver you up, take no thought beforehand what ye shall speak, neither do ye premeditate: but whatsoever shall be given you in that hour, that speak ye: for it is not ye that speak, but the Holy Ghost." ---
Mark 13:9,11

When my parents, Washington "Mickey" and Mildred Johnson became Adventists in mid-twentieth-century America, they broke every sociocultural, religious, and racial norm of the South. In the African American community, everyone was either a member of the African Methodist Episcopal (AME), Colored Methodist Episcopal (CME), Christ of God in Christ (COGIC), or the Baptist Church. The SDA Church didn't even register on the religious radar.

You must understand that beginning with slavery the church was the epic center of the African American community. It was the only arena where they could assume leadership, preach, teach, and socialize without the ugly face of Jim Crow reminding them of their inferior position in American society. Every major leader, Frederick Douglass, Booker T. Washington, Ella Baker, Fannie Lou Hamer, Rosa Parks, and Martin Luther King, Jr. were molded and shaped by the African American church.

Although African Americans were prohibited from entering the social mainstream of America, the church created its own social circle. It organized social and saving clubs, banquets, church picnics, fairs, choral societies, and fraternal orders. If you were not a part of the church, you were a social outcast. Upon acceptance of the gospel, my parents were no longer part of the social scene.

I remembered my father saying that family and friends, thought they had lost their minds because they were keeping the "Jewish Sabbath." The prevailing attitude was "I born a Sunday keeper and I will die a Sunday keeper." Although they sought to persuade my parents to return to the fold, they refused and because of their firm witness, my aunt and her family, my uncle and his family, grandmother, and several of their friends joined the church.

Now that my parents were Adventist their diet was radically changed. Southern culinary artistry dictated that almost every dish should be smothered in pork or cooked in lard. My father would buy a whole hog every month to make sure that the family had more than enough to eat. He prided himself on being an excellent provider.

Well, the day he accepted the gospel along with my mom, they decided that they would never again eat pork. It was a test because my father had just purchased a hog and their freezer was overflowing with pork chops, ribs, ham, bacon, etc. They had to decide, either they would eat all that was in their freezer and wait until next month to start an Adventist diet or they would trust God and be obedient. They didn't hesitate. They took all the pork and dumped it in the trash.

When one of the neighbors saw what my parents were doing, she called all her children and told them to bring sacks because Mickey and Mildred had lost their minds and were throwing away "good meat." My parents didn't prevent them from taking the meat, but they used it as an opportunity to share their faith. Later, they became Adventist and have remained faithful until this day.

The greatest challenge that my father encountered in his new faith was maintaining a job without working on the Sabbath. You see, we lived in the "Pittsburgh of the South," Birmingham, Alabama, and US Steel was the city's main employer. The belching furnaces of the Fairfield and Ensley Works created both a White and African American middle class. It was a cosmopolitan mix of poor immigrants, Italians, Lebanese, Poles, Irish, Russians, etc. who moved here in search of the American Dream and African Americans who fled rural Alabama, the poverty, and sharecropping to come to the "Magic City." If a man was industrious as my father, before long he could own a home, purchase a car, and send his children to private school.

Well like everything else, our middle-class lifestyle was severely tested. It started as a simple change in schedule because the plant was running 24/7 at full capacity, more workers were needed to work on Saturday. The superintendent of the plant, Mr. McClutchen told my father just as he was leaving on Friday afternoon, to be back Saturday morning at 7 a.m. because he was needed. "Sir, tomorrow is my Sabbath, I will be worshipping my Lord in church," but he added, "I can work 11-7 shift on Saturday night."

The workers listened intently to Mr. McCluthen's response, "Boy," he said threateningly, "if you don't show up you will see what will happen." His warning could be taken as a double threat. It meant two things, he could lose his job and put his family's future in jeopardy. Or even something more dreadful, he could be lynched by the Ku Klux Kan because my father had looked a White man straight in his eyes and defied his orders. Remember, only a few years had passed, since Emmett Till had been massacred because he allegedly whistled at a White woman.

Some of the workers were deeply concerned and tried to persuade my father to work the next day. They reminded him that he had a family, and he shouldn't put their lives in jeopardy because of the "Jewish Sabbath." While others reminded him, that he had a good life and risked losing everything because of his "weird religion." Others tried to fill him with fear, by reminding him of the deadly consequences he could incur, if he failed to obey the superintendent. He listened but firmly replied, "We ought to obey God, rather than man."

"Let him alone," some said, "he's crazy." Others asked, "who wants to bet that he will come in tomorrow?"

As the men lined up to bet, he quietly left. The Sabbath was before him and he and his family would honor God. Friday night devotion was bathed in prayer. Sabbath service was bathed in prayer as the congregation interceded for my father. By Sunday, my father was strengthened by the Spirit and was ready to return to work to accept the consequences.

At the appointed time, Monday morning, he arrived at 7 a.m. for the morning shift. Everyone stared at him but no one said a word. He went to punch in his timecard, but he didn't find it. That meant only one thing, he would have to go to the office to speak with Mr. McClutchen. So, he went with a prayer in his heart. As soon as he entered, the secretary informed him the executive directors of US Steel Corporation were waiting for him in the board room.

When he entered, seated at the table were US Steel's most powerful and influential leaders. God was at work and He reminded him of Mark 13. Mr. McClutchen presented the case against my father. Then one by one they tried to persuade my father to renounce his beliefs. Quoting 1 Timothy 5:8 they accused him of being worse than an infidel!

The Jewish lawyer, Stanley Levinson, in mocking tones, reminded him that he was a Jew and a Sabbath keeper, but he worked on Sabbath when the company needed him. "You're a Negro," he angrily said, "and how can you pretend to cherish the Sabbath more than a Jew?" After they had all spoken, he was given an opportunity to speak. The Holy Spirit spoke powerfully through my father. He gave them a clear and dynamic reason for his faith. When he had finished, they were speechless. After they recovered, they asked our pastor, Elder E.T. Mims, who they had invited for the express purpose of convincing, my father to work on the Sabbath, to speak. Pastor Mims fearlessly replied that, he was the one who had taught him the Sabbath truth and that he could not alter the commandments of the Lord. By now they were seething mad, they fired my father on the spot and asked them both to get out!

Upon leaving the office, the Holy Spirit revealed to him that he would be rehired the same day. He returned home and waiting at the door was my mom with a big smile on her face, and the phone in her hand, it was US Steel and they wanted to rehire him and added a raise. They said they were deeply impressed by my father's courage of conviction and wished that all their workers would exhibit such integrity and honesty. God is amazing!

Lord, give me the courage to unwaveringly stand for You, even if it means standing alone because I know that You are with me and You alone will bring me out victorious. Amen!

Stephanie Johnson-Dingome

God's Word

Thy word is a lamp unto my feet, and a light unto my path.
Psalms 119:105 KJV.

From a young age, I was taught the stories from the Bible, like how David, and Goliath, the three Hebrew boys, crossed the Red Sea. And at first, that's all that they were, stories that I was forced to learn. As time went by, and I matured, they became something much greater. I started reading for understanding and even for pleasure.

The Books of the Bible became letters from a dear friend. They would speak of what He's been up to over the years, His hope, advice, His character and His feelings for me, and His plans for the future. Over the years, I've been able to discern His voice. The times that I listen, He's been able to keep me out of trouble and the times I don't, I've been assured of His eagerness to forgive. We've had quite a few arguments and even wrestling matches on occasion. But I've found that when I submit to Him, what I have lost is greatly outweighed by what I have gained.

Dear Lord, please help me to choose to get to know You as well as I can through Your words of love and guidance.

Christine Thompson

Seeking God Early in the Morning

"I have set the LORD always before me because He is at my right hand, I shall not be moved." Psalms 16:8

Rising early these days to do my a.m. workout is not an easy thing to do. However, this new thing is allowing me to put my God first every morning as I rise. I travel about thirty minutes to my trainer studio, so that's thirty minutes in the early morning of total commuting with God, listening to his word, praying to Him as I drive to and from the studio. Thirty minutes of listening to scriptures, praying to God to lead my day, direct my steps, thoughts, hands, and ears. Giving God your day from the beginning of the day, declaring this is His day and He has blessed me with it. I am choosing to be happy in the day, and rejoicing and being glad for the day, this four o'clock hour and every hour of the day.

My thirst for life and the opportunity to open my heart and my mind, and to use all the resources He provides for that day wisely. I have discovered that I am able to openly pray for everyone I encounter daily, sending peace, joy, and love to them. Praying for health, happiness, and prosperity for their household.

Connecting with my Father early in the morning really sets my whole day in motion. As I speak over the individuals, I am amazed at the peacefulness that I also enjoy. Choosing to spend time with my Father in heaven, my Father knows I am depending on Him for my day to go right and guide me through all my business encounters and transactions.

My mood, attitude, energy, and level of calmness are reflected positively as I go about the day in a grateful and thankful manner. At the end of the day, when I reflect on the day, it is always one of gratitude and success as I count it. I see the things I accomplish and the awesomeness of God as He works through me for His glory. I complete my day by writing ten things I am thankful and grateful for, and every time I do that, I can recall those ten things that I was thankful and grateful for. It allows me to see the smallest and least significant things to reflect and to thank God for it. I clearly see the thing that I would normally take for granted.

Seeking God early in the morning helps me keep my eyes on Jesus all day long. Prayer, scripture readings, and daily meditation is the way to Jesus Christ, it moves us closer and closer to Him. Seek God with all your heart, come with an open mind. You will find Him when you seek him with all your heart, He is waiting for you. He is ready to listen, and He cares for you.

He LOVES you! Seeking God early refreshes you for the whole day's journey, no matter what the day brings forth, God got you. It will amaze you how peaceful and exciting your day is when you turn it over to Him. Whatever comes, God's got it.

Our Father I approach Your throne today for all that You have done in my life with sincere gratitude. I am thankful that I am filled with life this new day. I know that I can call on Your name, the name above all name to guide me today in the things I must do. I commit and surrender the day fully to You in Jesus' name I pray, Amen!

Susan Gooding-Liburd

I am Strengthened through Christ' Strength

Trusting in God

"I can do all things through Christ who strengthens me."
Philippians 4:13

This is one of my favorite scriptures in the Bible. In fact, how can you not make this Scripture one of your favorite, uplifting, soul stirring, take-on-any challenge in the world promise? Paul wrote this promise at some of the most difficult trials of his life. His experience allowed him to write boldly, "I can do all things through Christ that gives me strength."

This was the Scripture I repeated as I completed my doctoral course work and entered the dissertation phase. I had some apprehension as previous students referred to this phase as a daunting task, mainly because it is the largest piece of work in fulfilling a doctoral degree. Notwithstanding, the challenges, I planned to do a specific proportion of my study every day.

Understanding that this is a rigorous research project, I followed the dissertation outline at Walden University to ensure I stayed focused on selecting relevant literature, ensured the research question, statement of the problem and purpose of the study aligned. As I delved into the first three chapters, notably, the extensive literature review, I recognized the passion I had for my topic. This passion propelled my energy, sustained my efforts, and helped me endured all the frustrations that arose.

In my pre-dissertation class, my professor told us that he only knew one student that completed his dissertation in one year. He said, normally, students take 3 to 10 years to complete their dissertation. Immediately, I began to repeat this Scripture, "I can do all things through Christ who strengthens me." I knew beyond a shadow of a doubt that I can complete my dissertation within one year, with the help of the Lord. To say the least, it was rough and challenging, and many times I thought of giving up, but words of Paul came forcefully, you can do all things through Christ.

Subsequently, to the completion of the first chapter, one of my brothers passed away. It was extremely difficult to stay focus. During the next several chapters, my son-in-law underwent several surgeries. Looking back, it was only the grace of God that kept me. At the end of my dissertation, my youngest brother passed away. It was a very difficult time as I mourned the loss of two very dear brothers in one year. Even though I am delighted to say that I completed my dissertation in 11 months. I am aware it wasn't me that did it, but it was accomplished through God's strength. At that moment, I realized that the strength of Almighty God reaches down to our pain, our trials, and intense moments and carry us through when we see no way out.

James said it best "Consider it pure joy, my brothers, whenever you face trials of many kinds, because you know that the testing of your faith develops perseverance. Perseverance must finish its work so that you may be mature and complete, not lacking anything." James 1: 2-4.

We are granted the strength by God to navigate the trials, endure the hardships, and grow. Let our faith blossom through these difficult times as we grow in His grace.

Eternal Father give us the strength to carry us through the most difficult times of our lives. We recognize that we cannot do it on our own. Through Your merit, show us Your will and lead us to the Rock that is higher than I. Help us to boldly embrace the Scripture: "I can do all things through Christ that gives me strength" In the precious name of Jesus. Amen!

Dr. Donna Barrett

Faith Works

Now, Faith is the substance of things hoped for the evidence of things not seen. Hebrew 11:1

When we are faced with a now situation, we need a now faith to pull us out and this is not an easy thing to do. We know that God is an ever-present help in the time of trouble, but we panic, we give in to frustration, we let fear take over. When trouble, sickness, financial difficulties, etc. come our way, we are to hold fast to our faith in God. For God is faithful.

Now Faith means at that very same time as you're praying you must see the answer, which is the thing that you are hoping or praying for in your mind's eyes. You must VISION the answer as if it is already received. When you do this, it becomes the evidence of things hoped or prayed for. When you have evidence, you have proof, meaning it is shown that it is present.

I was 23 weeks pregnant and went to the hospital to get a scan. Upon getting the scan, I was rushed into the maternity ward where I was told I had no water. My baby was in the vaginal walls and that I was having a miscarriage. I was told by my doctor that the hospital will only try and save a 24-week baby, however, mine happen to be 23weeks. Now through a prophet and through the word, God had already told me I was carrying a prophet, so my faith kicked in. I said a prophet and a miscarriage does not add up and I'm not having a miscarriage, my baby shall live and not die. I told the doctor if you need one more week, I will stay in the hospital, but my baby will live. My son was born on the day that made the 24 weeks. He came out kicking although he was only weighing one pound. John had many challenges but all that the doctor said could've gone wrong because of my age at the time, did not happen. John was born on October 2, 2009. I was 47. John is now 11 years old and has never been back in the hospital.

Dear Heavenly Father, I receive the answer to my prayer by faith, knowing that it is already done, for Your word says when I pray whatever I ask for in Jesus' name believe I receive and I will have it, so thank You, Father, for Your Ever-increasing Faith in Jesus name I pray. Amen!

Gwen Greenslade

Serving God Through Serving Others

But do not forget to do good, and to share, for with such sacrifices God is well pleased

Hebrews 13:16)

Many people have the misconception that serving others is limited to pastors and other leaders. In fact, the Bible says everyone is called to serve God by serving others. We are our brother's keepers and when a brother/sister is in need it is our duty to help fill that need. God has blessed us with gifts, talents, and resources so we are well equipped to bless others.

Serving others reveals a bond between us. It reflects the Love of God, provides an opportunity to meet a physical need, and at the same time share our faith with those whom we interact. It's a time to let our lights shine. We are tasked with putting the needs of others ahead of our own needs. Let us be intentional about this; there is a powerful feeling of satisfaction and purpose when we can make a difference in someone else's life.

Serving to be noticed is not something that pleases God, so let us serve without expecting anything in return. All the glory belongs to God.

God doesn't just want to work through us, he wants to work in us, to draw us closer to Him. As we strive to be more like Him, let's reflect on the parable of the goats and the sheep. Let us feed the hungry, visit the sick, and clothe those who are naked. Let us be obedient so we can hear Him say "inasmuch as you have done it to one of the least of my brethren, you did it to me." (Matthew 25:40)

I encourage you to befriend the friendless, be the champion of the underdog. Let us seek out the poor and marginalized, the lost and lonely, and love them the way Jesus loves us.

Almighty God, we praise Your name, You alone are worthy of our praise. We thank You for your beloved Son who came to earth and exemplified love and service to others. We are grateful that He came to serve and not to be served, setting an example for us. We pray, Dear Lord, for eyes to see others as You see us. Help us not to be selective in whom we serve. May Your life of love and service be our daily guide. May we give our time, love, effort, and our resources as You so freely gave, and may our acts of kindness transform the lives of those we serve. We thank You for all that You are and for all that You do. Thank You for hearing our prayers. In Jesus' name, we pray. Amen!

Dorrett Gonzales

His Purpose for My Life - Yield to His Will

A man's heart deviseth his way: but the LORD directeth his steps." Proverbs 16:9 (KJV)

I had the fortune or misfortune of having to take care of my ailing mother for years. Yes, I was fortunate because I loved caring for her. No, it was unfortunate for I had little to no time for leisure. The year was 2012. I was deputy student representative while I was pursuing a certificate in educational leadership. I was expected to attend a function given that the student representative was ill. I was determined that I would go that Saturday night.

Was it God's will? I did not know, but I wanted to attend the event. I forgot that the Word of God admonishes us that we should not say that we will go here or there without consultation with God. In James 4:15, we are told, "For that ye ought to say, If the Lord will, we shall live and do this, or that." Having not consulted and having not been granted the Lord's blessing, I started to dress. Suddenly, like Saul on the road to Damascus, I was struck in the eye by something unknown. My eyes suddenly became gritty and started to water. I could neither see well nor drive to the function. I spent the night instead of at a local health clinic seeking medical attention.

The lesson was learned: *Proverbs 16:9 - A man's heart deviseth his way: but the LORD directed his steps. Have you, like I did, been thinking that you simply had to decide what you wanted to do and just do it. If you have declared yourself to be on God's side, then think again,*" Ye are not your own, for ye are bought with a price: therefore, glorify God in your body, and in your spirit, which is God's (1 Corinthians 6:19-20). Place all your plans, thoughts, and fears before Him. He will guide you into all truth if you learn to listen to His voice and simply obey it.

Heavenly Father, thank You for being the guide of my life. Help me to remember to acknowledge You in all my ways so that You can direct my path. In Jesus' name, Amen.

Debbie Bovell

The Power of the Word

For the word of God is quick, and powerful, and sharper than any two-edged sword. Heb. 4:12

I grew up reading and listening to Bible stories about the power of God's Word and felt awe at the mission spotlights presented in Sabbath School or other places. I read and believed and loved the Word all my life, but its power became more real to me when I began to experience the climacteric, or what is commonly known as menopause.

The Word of God became my strength and stay to a greater degree during this time, than any other. When anxiety and palpitations presented, my heart retained or returned to its calm through the words of the prophet Isaiah. I could hear Jehovah saying to me, "Fear thou not; for I am with thee be not dismayed; for I am thy God: I will strengthen thee; yea, I will help thee; yea, I will uphold thee with the right hand of my righteousness" Isa. 41:10.

I recall distinctly, a Sunday afternoon when I was home alone. I was in a safe environment. I was enjoying myself, when suddenly and for no apparent reason, my heart began to race in my chest. It was very unnerving, and I did not know how to stop it. I reached for a devotional that I loved, and the Spirit led me to Psalm 27: 14, "Wait on the Lord: be of good courage, and He shall strengthen thine heart: wait, I say, on the Lord." I believed the Word and before long, the pounding in my chest subsided.

The Scriptures fast became my place of comfort. As each day presented, I committed myself to God as soon as I felt life in me. Whatever promise was given for the day I wrote in a pocket-sized notebook, carried it with me, and memorized it. I can still hear myself climbing the stairs to my class, reciting, "The eternal God is thy refuge, and underneath are the everlasting arms" Deut. 33: 27. These promises enlarged my faith in an ever-loving, ever-present Creator. I knew that His word cannot change and will not return to Him void but shall accomplish the thing He pleases and will prosper in the thing where it is sent.

Are you in a place of unwelcome change today? Is there a health crisis? The COVID-19 pandemic presents much uncertainty. Yet, God's Word is certain. Not maybe certain or will be certain, but is certain. You can trust Him when He assures you, "I the Lord do keep it; I will water it every moment: lest any hurt it, I will keep it night and day." Isaiah 27:3.

Dear God, You are my place of assurance when all appears uncertain. You have a divine surveillance system over my life. I trust Your Word. It stands fast forever. I will not fear. Nothing can prevent Your word from coming true. I know that I am secure in Your Word today.

Jean Trotman

Hope in Uncertainty

Why am I discouraged? Why is my heart so sad? I will put my hope in God! I will praise him again—my Savior and my God!
Psalm. 43:5 NLT

Sometimes when life seems chaotic and everything seems dim, it is easy to lose hope.

It was 2008, the stock market had just crashed, and like millions of Americans, everything seemed grim. I was struggling to keep up with my mortgage payments and I finally defaulted. Would I lose my home? Where would I go? What does one do in a situation like that? I sought the Lord earnestly for guidance and He gave me the strength to endure. More than that, He would allow me to stay in my home for an extended period. Praise His name! What a mighty God we serve!

But then came the notices, foreclosure notices, court hearings, the 20 days to vacate notice, and finally, the house was foreclosed. Sadly, I moved out, rented an apartment, and thanked God for the years He had given me in my home, and moved on in faith. I wasn't sure where God would lead me next, but I knew that He was in control. He had always been there through my struggles and He wasn't about to leave me now. I wasn't ready for how He would lead.

One day, out of the blue, I received a phone call with a proposal to help me get my house back. It was now time to stand still and see the salvation of the Lord. Within two months of that phone call, I was back in my home. All my arrears were paid off and I now had a fresh start. What a miracle it was!

I am still amazed at how wonderful God is. He takes care of His children. He is still a miracle-working God. When all else fails, rest assured that God will be there for you. Philippians 4:6-7 says "Do not be anxious about anything, but in everything by prayer and supplication with thanksgiving let your requests be made known to God. And the peace of God, which surpasses all understanding, will guard your hearts and your minds in Christ Jesus."

Our God knows our every need and is always ever close to us. He has promised that He will never leave us nor forsake us. (Hebrews 13:5) I am reminded of the poem: Footprints in the Sand; particularly the last verse "My precious child, I love you and will never leave you never, ever, during your trials and testings. When you saw only one set of footprints, it was then that I carried you." When it seems like you are all alone, know that God is carrying you.

In this world of constant uncertainty, you can always find hope in God. Don't give up! I had read the bible many times and seen how God had worked in the lives of bible characters but now it was my turn to experience Him. James 1:2-6 says "Count it all joy, my brothers, when you meet trials of various kinds, for you know that the testing of your faith produces steadfastness. And let steadfastness have its full effect, that you may be perfect and complete, lacking in nothing. If any of you lacks wisdom, let him ask God, who gives generously to all without reproach, and it will be given him. But let him ask in faith, with no doubting, for the one who doubts is like a wave of the sea that is driven and tossed by the wind."

Thank You Lord, for Your many blessings in my life. Those that I can or cannot see. Help me to always know that You are with me. Help me to put all my hope and trust in You. Whenever I get discouraged or feel hopeless, may Your Holy Spirit remind me of your leading in my life. May this experience help me to never lose sight that You are an on-time God. When it seems as though all hope is gone, may I be reminded that hope is found in You! in Jesus' name, Amen.

Michell Buttler

Thanksgiving

"Obey these instructions as a lasting ordinance for you and your descendants. When you enter the land that the LORD will give you as he promised, observe this ceremony. And when your children ask you, 'What does this ceremony mean to you?' then tell them, 'It is the Passover sacrifice to the LORD, who passed over the houses of the Israelites in Egypt and spared our homes when he struck down the Egyptians.'" Then the people bowed down and worshiped. Exodus 12:24-28

This was the instruction given by Almighty Lord to the Israelites to celebrate the Passover each year in remembrance of the day when the Lord spared the Israelites from being struck down along with the Egyptians. They were also instructed to tell their children about it. This was so that the Israelites would remember that the Lord brought them out of Egypt with a mighty hand and this, in turn, would bring about a grateful spirit to the Lord for what He did for them, and as they taught it to their children, it would increase their own faith in the struggles they faced day to day, each year, that the Lord who kept them safe from the Death Angel and also provided for them by causing the Egyptians to have favor on them to give the departing Israelites gold and silver and clothing for their Journey (Exodus 12:35), was able to provide for them and protect them forever.

Today let's celebrate the victories the Lord Almighty gives us big or small. Write it down in a book and when you feel anxious or worried or tensed, read the book and give thanks to the Lord for past victories and you will notice that your worries slowly fade away and you will have the faith to pray and believe that God is in control and He can change your situation.

Father God, I thank You for all the blessings in my life big and small. May I always be reminded of your Goodness in my life so I may worship and serve You in peace.

Sausana Abraham

Amazing Grace

By the righteousness of one man the free gift came upon all men unto justification of life. Romans 5:8

Covid-19 has brought desperation, loneliness, sickness and death upon all, when it entered our shores in 2020. The outlook wasn't good; all had a foreboding mindset. The panacea was to build and strengthen the immune system. I vigorously committed my stomach to that notable path, but very soon it's displeasure grew progressively worse, and it's daily picketing forced me to retreat. I landed in a doctor's office who loaded me with a barrage of medications; a list of diagnostic tests; and verbal and written instructions. Two to three months later there was not much improvement and I decided to seek Divine Intervention. My family and friends were enlisted in this vigil activity.

Due to my progressive weight loss, my emotions got the better of me at times. I was not doing well, but worse of all, I felt the ever-increasing space between myself and God. God was not hearing my prayers! I was not hearing from Him! I was not feeling Him! I was alone! I felt dejected! I felt empty! I felt rejected by my God! To top it all off, my mind began to generate an awareness of my sins and they were weighty; even after praying. I was left with no security and became unsure of my salvation. The question that plagued my mind then, was "*If Jesus should come now, would I be lost?*" The answer pressed home menacingly, "*I am not ready.*"

The fear of my possible loss condition inundated and cascaded my mind and I cried out to God, asking for mercy, forgiveness, and for an assurance of His presence in my crisis. All this transpired on a Friday evening as I was preparing Sabbath lunch and getting ready to complete other activities.

As I continued with my preparations, my tears flowed and then subsided. Suddenly, a thought flashed in my head. It was dramatic, I stopped and blinked a few times. Is this for real? I felt as if a light bulb switched on in my head. It flashed these words "*It is Satan that wants you to believe that you are lost. Jesus died for your sins, and you have a merciful Father who hears and forgives if you confess and forsake your sins.*" This truth appears novel! Such good news! Refresh with such living waters, I now understood what Calvary really meant.

Brethren, I let loose on Satan! With tearful eyes, marching up and down in the house, I gave him his Marching Orders. I told him he is a liar, a thief, and a deceiver. With tears streaming down my cheeks and nose drippings in sympathy with the flow, I fixed him that day! I declared that God is my Father and reminded him that Jesus is in the Heavenly sanctuary pleading on my behalf. "*Satan I am not lost, get thee behind me.*" Coming from my lips was a promise to God and a request to help me to trust Him. I know He heard every word and He saw every tear that Friday evening.

Today, I continue to pray and thank God for rescuing me from the powerful Jaws of Satan and for giving me the assurance that He is with me.

Thank You Lord and please Jesus remind me that I am Yours. I love you Lord! Amen!

Marcia Holness

Forgiving Others- A Requirement

If we confess our sins, he is faithful and just to forgive us our sins, and to cleanse us from all unrighteousness.1 John 1:9 KJV

Have you heard the expression "the world is unkind?" Have you ever experienced unkindness, unfair treatment, disloyalty? I am sure most of us, if not all of us, can recall having been unkindly or unfairly treated, or having been let down by a close, trusted friend, even by a family member, a spouse, someone from whom we expected better. Many of us have experienced hurts that have left deep scars.

Recently, I was conversing with a young sister who a few years ago had moved to another area far from mine, so I hadn't seen her for quite a while. I was very pleasantly surprised by her phone call. As we were chatting, she said to me: "*I will NEVER forgive my father for what he has done to my mother.*" That is a seriously dangerous statement, especially coming from the lips of a professed practicing Seventh-day Adventist Christian. Sadly, we do not even realize how serious such an expression is when it comes to our salvation. Too often, we hold grudges and express such feelings of animosity and give reasons for the enemy of our soul to exult and ensure we keep in that frame of mind. On hearing such, I believe he says: "Yea, that is it, do not forgive, do not relate, you have been too badly hurt, avoid, cut all ties!" The more we allow these words to escape our lips, the more bitter we become towards the individual, we avoid any contact, anger surges just at the mention of the name of the person, the whole experience comes back alive, and the anger roots goes deeper and deeper. Does that sound familiar?

In Matthew 6: 12, 14, 15; 18: 35 Jesus admonishes us to forgive; that is a requirement to obtain forgiveness for our own sin and answer to our prayers. This is easier said than done if we try to do it in our own strength because the natural inclination is to hold grudges, to retaliate. But thanks be to God, Jesus stands ready to help; and when we recognize the serious implications of such an attitude, our helplessness to overcome it and turn to Him, talk to Him daily, every time something triggers the reminder of the hurt and refer it back to Him, He is true and faithful to His promise of help, we can overcome. In our quiet moments, as we sincerely pray for the individual mentioning him by name to Jesus, we can gradually come out of that mold. Determine not to accommodate its return and entrust it to Jesus every time, we can, and we will be relieved and victorious.

There is absolutely no hope of getting into the kingdom unless our sins are forgiven--ALL OUR SINS must be blotted out, our robes must be washed in the blood of the Lamb.

Let us look at Revelation 22: 1, 2 "And He shewed me a pure river of water of life, clear as crystal, proceeding out of the throne of God and of the Lamb. In the midst of the street of it, and on either side of the river, was there the tree of life, which bare twelve manner of fruits, and yielded her fruit every month; and the leaves of the tree were for the healing of the nations." Can we afford to miss out on these blissful promises? Philippians 4: 13 assures us that we can do ALL things through Christ Jesus our LORD." Jesus is standing ready eager to pilot you through. Why not let Him in? Do not delay, talk to Him today, NOW. Tomorrow may be too late!

Forgiving does not necessarily mean reconciliation and getting back where we were initially; it does not mean that the individual has done no wrong. It means that we are allowing ourselves to be released from a heavy burden, a burden that is much too heavy on our shoulders, a burden that is crushing us, a burden that will eventually cost us our salvation. Won't you let Jesus do it for you today, won't you give Him the helm and let Him pilot you?

Father, I understand clearly the serious implications of holding on to unforgiveness, but Lord, I am weak, I cannot do it on my own, I have been so badly hurt. I am giving you my hurt, my deep scars. I do not want to nurture it anymore. Take it, Father, and relieve me of this crushing burden. Please, forgive me for not forgiving all these years. I have been hurt so deeply, Lord, the scars are still fresh, but in your strength, I believe I can, and I am willing to forgive now. Help me, please, in Jesus' name. AMEN!

Josiane Jones

Forgiveness

Ephesians 3:20 "Now to Him who is able to do immeasurably more than all we ask or think, according to the power that worketh in us."

Ever felt the burning heat of betrayal or the pain of a broken heart? Ever thought that if you could only hear the words "I'm sorry," then everything would go back to normal, and it wouldn't hurt so much anymore. But what if I am sorry never comes and things don't ever go back to how it was, does that mean that we can never move on?

Jesus understands what we go through when these things happen. Imagine the Savior of the world came and was rejected by the very people He came to save. They spat on Him, despised and beat Him, they crucified Him, yet He never received a "thank you" nor "I'm sorry". If Jesus went through all of that and felt the same pain we do now, what better person to learn from and walk us through the healing process than Him. Jesus is the best person to take as a mentor in this regard. Hebrews 4:15 tells us that we have a high priest who understands our weaknesses because he faced all the same feelings we did yet did not sin. So again, the question is asked what if we never hear "I'm sorry "and what if the friendship never gets back to the way it used to be, how would we feel?

Before Jesus left, He told us that just as He overcame, we too can do the same. Not that we would overcome on our own, but He left us a comforting presence who has all authority to speak and act on His behalf; only then can we truly be ok and carry on even if we don't ever hear that apology that we oftentimes tend to wait on or if that friendship we had invested so much time and memories in doesn't ever look the same. "No harm no foul" the world often says yet hold grudges. However, as Christians, we ought to let our mantra be "no harm just love," as if the wrong never happened in the first place. How can this be possible you may ask? Only through Jesus.

Dear Lord, please help me to forgive and love the ones who have caused me harm. Show me your ways so that I won't try in my own human efforts because I know I will fail.

Kaye Ann Clarke

Trusting in the Lord

Trust the Lord with all thine heart and lean not unto your own understanding, in all thy ways acknowledge Him and He shall direct thy path. Psalm 27:14 declares: "Wait on the Lord; Be of good courage, And He shall strengthen your heart; Wait, I say on the Lord."

Psalm 62: 2&5 – God is my Rock and my Salvation; He is my Defense. Another translation stated, "He is my Fortress, I will never be shaken, or I shall not be greatly moved." And one of my favorites is from Isaiah 40:31 "But those who wait on the Lord, shall renew their strength; They shall mount up with wings like eagles; They shall run, and not be weary; They shall walk and not faint." Psalm 37: 5-7 "Commit your way to the Lord; trust in Him and He will do this; He shall bring your righteousness as the light, and your justice as the noonday," another translation, "Your reward will shine like the dawn, your vindication like the noonday sun."

These were some of the scriptures I repeated after the surgeon called and said they must take my daughter into emergency surgery. The doctor said, "I can't stay on the phone with you, this is a life and death situation." Several days after my daughter delivered her first child, she was diagnosed with a flesh-eating bacterium (Necrotizing Fasciitis). The doctor stated, "the bacteria is eating her tissues; up her stomach walls and down her leg. We are unsure of what is going on. What is clear is that we must perform emergency surgery right away." At that moment, I hung up the phone, screamed, and said Lord, I leave everything in your capable hands. I trust you, Lord, I believe in you, I worship You!!

My daughter spent four weeks in intensive care with multiple tubes strung from different parts of her body. She was swollen from head to toe. She was intubated and placed on a ventilator to help with breathing. She was taken to the operating room seven times for surgery. At the end of the surgeries, a wound vac was recommended to help close the wound. These were some difficult days; however, I knew beyond the shadow of a doubt that God was in control. As I look back on how our miracle-working God intervened, I am humbled, amazed, and thrilled all at the same time, to experience the power of God in such a magnificent way. After seven days in a coma and several surgeries, I am happy to note that the surgeries were successful, and my daughter is doing well. We serve a mighty and awesome God! Whatever challenges you are going through, trust in God to carry you through. He can do more than you can ask or imagine.

Loving Father, thank You for showing up in times of distress when I cry out to You. You responded in ways that only You can. My trust is unshakable in You. You reminded us in Your Word, Psalm 125:1 "Those who trust in the Lord are like Mount Zion. Which cannot be moved but abides forever." Continue to guide and protect me in Jesus' name, Amen! – Dr. Donna Barrett

Trust

Trust the Lord with all your heart and lean not on your own understanding. Proverbs 3:5

My uncle got married to a wonderful woman. As a child, I enjoyed watching them together. They did almost everything together, including building a business. My whole family loved her dearly, she was like a guardian angel in our lives. Where advice was needed, she provided it, whether social, emotional, financial, or spiritual.

As children, my cousins and I would often visit my aunt and uncle. It was such a joy to be with them especially since strong, wholesome relationships seem very rare. She took care of us as if we were her own children. Before I had the chance to experience puberty, I remembered having many discussions with her about it. She later bought me a book on the subject, I suspect she did so just in case I had other questions. She was that type of person, very caring, and knows just what to say and do in different situations. As I grew from a child to a young woman, she continued to nurture me. When I announced I was getting married, again she provided wise counsel and bought me yet another book on healthy marriage and relationships.

Although we lived in two different countries, we still maintained our connection. It became a tradition for me to speak to my aunt and uncle every Friday night. Those were delightful discussions that were honest and full of joy. Before I even got married, I hoped that my relationship would be as wonderful as theirs. Each time I visited my family, I would stay with my aunt and uncle. It was a joy to be in their company and we continued to have wholesome and healthy conversations.

Then one day I received a phone call that my aunt had cancer. I was devastated. I prayed and prayed, fasted and prayed, prayed and prayed, and prayed and fasted some more. At one point it seems as if she was getting better, then she took a turn for the worse. I remembered the story of Lazarus and I pleaded with God, "If you can raise Lazarus from the dead, you can surely make my aunt better". Other stories came to mind such as Jairus' daughter, the Shunammite woman's son, the widow of Zarephath's son, the widow of Nain's son, and others who were healed from sickness and diseases. "God, if you heal my aunt, so many people would know about you and would come to praise and glorify your name."

My prayers seem like they were in vain because I awoke one morning to the terrible news that she died. I cried like a baby for what seemed like an eternity. I began to question God "She was such a lovely person; why did you take her away from us? She was kind and loving and she helped so many people, could you not have spared her life?" The pain I felt was unbearable.

During this dark period, I was reminded of Isaiah 55:8 "For my thoughts are not your thoughts, neither are your ways my ways, declares the Lord." I was also reminded to trust in God because He knows what He is doing. He is our one and only wise and true God. I know that if I am faithful, I will once again see my aunt at that great reunion in the sky.

Dear Heavenly Father, thank You for the reminder that I should trust in You, even when I cannot see a clear path. Amen

Ann Marie Troupe-Afflick

Courage For The Crisis

"I hereby command you: Be strong and courageous; do not be frightened or dismayed, for the Lord your God is with you wherever you go." Joshua 1:9

We live in a world filled with chaos, problems, sorrow, gloom, sadness, hurt, natural disasters and the list goes on and on. We may ask questions like; how do I maintain courage during these crises? Will I crumble under pressure? How do I go on? Is there a secret to live a life of faith when my whole world is crumbling around me? How can I be courageous when my whole world is falling apart? The truth is, we are surrounded by a mountain of fear, anxiety, and worry. Even though we are surrounded and bombarded by these challenges we take courage in the fact that nothing takes God by surprise, He is always there to carry us through the darkest and bleakest moments of our life. The dictionary definition of Courage is "the ability to do something that frightens one, it is "Strength in the face of pain or grief" and it is "the quality of mind or spirit that enables a person to face difficulty, danger, and pain without fear"

COVID-19 has added an extra layer to all the other challenges in our life. We have real struggles and real pain; we face legitimate concerns every day. Bad things happen to good people. Real problems do occur, usually daily. People don't act the way they ought to. Relationships falter and sometimes fail. There is potential for crisis all around us. And there are certainly things that require concern and action on our part. However, our focus should never be on the crisis on hand, but on our Creator, Redeemer, Sustainer, and Friend. He knows everything. He is an expert in chaotic situations. He is the only One you can call on. So, the question is "How can we maintain courage in crisis?" Is it possible? Well, let me share 4 very important principles that will allow you to maintain "Courage In The Crisis"

1. **You Must Have Faith in God!**
2. **You Must Trust in the Lord!**
3. **You Must Be Still!**
4. **You Must Fast and Pray!**

When your world crumbles around you, and it will, the call from Scriptures is: "***Be strong and courageous; do not be frightened or dismayed, for the Lord your God is with you wherever you go.***" Have Faith, Trust in God, Be Still, Pray and Fast—not because you are the most composed person in the face of disaster, not because "you've seen it all." But because of what you know about God. Be still because He is the Alpha and

Omega, be still because He is the First and the Last, be still because He is our Sustainer, Redeemer, and Friend. Be still because He knows your wants and your needs, be still because He can do more than you can ask or imagine. Be still because He will fight for you. Be still because He will open the doors and windows that no man can shut. Be still because He can close any door or window that man cannot shut. Trust Him because He is the Great, I AM, He is the Bright and Morning Star. He is the Rock of Ages. He is in control!

Oh, Heavenly Father, how thankful we are to have a Savior who looks out for our best interest. Increase our faith, help us to trust You more, help us to be still so You can work on us and give us an obedient Spirit to fast and pray. In times of uncertainty, let our faith be larger than a mustard seed. We are relying on Your mercies and ever-flowing grace to help us to Be Still during chaotic situations. In the name of Jesus. Amen!

Dr. Donna Barrett

Trusting in God

"You keep him in perfect peace whose mind is stayed on you because he trusts in you. Trust in the Lord forever, for the Lord God is an everlasting rock." Isaiah 26: 3-4

Father, don't you see how tired I am? I need a vacation. I am on this treadmill called "work", and I cannot get off. Can't you send me on vacation to a deserted island with a beautiful beach and someone to cook my meals? NO talking, NO problems to solve, just silence

This had been my constant prayer each morning while driving to work, before dawn. Well, my prayers were heard and answered that same year! But, not quite in the way, I had imagined. For some time now I had been having digestive problems. One by one, I'd been eliminating foods from my diet. The foods I could no longer digest. So, like any good Caribbean born, I started myself on a regimen of herbs and porridge, to soothe my angry stomach.

Eventually, when it became unbearable, I gave in and set an appointment for an endoscopy to be done. Of course, I knew they would find nothing, and my medical records would remain clean. "Well,", I reasoned, "if I am going in to do the endoscopy, I might as well submit to the dreaded colonoscopy".

May 11, 2018. The date of my procedure had arrived. I had accomplished all the necessary pre-procedure steps. My sister dropped me off at the hospital, accompanied by my Mom. The assistants were kind and helpful, explaining everything, each step of the way. Before long, I was waking up post-op, trying to focus, and acclimate to the reality around me. The doctor came in. He told me what the endoscopy revealed. I had chronic gastritis. But he assured me that it would heal on its own. "Nothing to worry about" he smiled. Though I hadn't expected bad news, his words were reassuring all the same. The next milestone was the colonoscopy.

Someone's voice was telling me that they found a mass in my ascending colon. "YOU HAVE CANCER." Was he speaking to me? "No," I thought, "Someone else must be in the room too," Slowly, I turned my head to find this person who was just diagnosed with cancer, but no one else was there! No! it just could not be me! The doctor left, and the nurse came in. "What do I tell my mother?" I asked helplessly "Do not say the word 'cancer'. Just say there is a large polyp needing to be removed," she replied

My sister came to pick us up, and I managed to tell her at a moment when my mom was out of earshot. She cried all the way home. That night when I went to bed. I looked around my room with an empty feeling; Of all the things I had acquired, nothing could be of comfort to me. Then a verse in Ecclesiastes 1 came to mind. "Vanity of vanities, saith the Preacher, vanity of vanities; all is vanity. What profit hath a man of all his labor which he taketh under the sun."

"Dear God, this problem is bigger than me. I cannot solve it. One thing I have decided: I refuse to spend a single night worrying about this. I will do everything I can to help my body to heal. It is now your problem - I am giving it to You. Here Lord, take it. Good night."

Aldyth Roach

Faith

When the angel of the Lord appeared to Gideon, he said, "The Lord is with you, mighty warrior. Pardon me, my lord," Gideon replied, "but if the Lord is with us, why has all this happened to us? Where are all his wonders that our ancestors told us about when they said, 'Did not the Lord bring us up out of Egypt?' But now the Lord has abandoned us and given us into the hand of Midian." The Lord turned to him and said, "Go in the strength you have and save Israel out of Midian's hand. Am I not sending you? "Pardon me, my lord," Gideon replied, "but how can I save Israel? My clan is the weakest in Manasseh, and I am the least in my family." The Lord answered, "I will be with you, and you will strike down all the Midianites, leaving none   Judges 6: 12-16

When the angel appeared to Gideon and called him 'Mighty Warrior' in Judges Chapter 6, Gideon did not think that about himself nor had he done any mighty deeds till then and he felt he was the least in his clan. But the Lord saw him as a Mighty Warrior and he assured Gideon that He would be with Gideon and that Gideon would strike down the Midianites. All Gideon needed was the presence of God and Gideon believed him after the sign that the angel of the Lord showed him.

Imagine the victories in our lives, if we could just have faith to see ourselves as God sees us. He sees us a mighty warrior because the presence of the Lord would always be with us to help us through. I did my engineering in electronics and communication. An average student, after some years I was searching for a job, I was fasting and praying for it too and I got a job in one of the best offshore banks in the world. I was so shocked that I even got the job in that bank even though I fasted and prayed for a job as I thought I was mediocre. But God saw something in me that I didn't see at that time and the Holy Spirit reminded me of Gideon in the Bible And so I started searching the scriptures for what word of God told me about myself and my purpose. It completely changed me. I started praying for wisdom and knowledge and understanding and skill just like God granted to people in the Bible and God completely changed me. Friends from my childhood and college can attest to that fact.

I challenge you today to see yourself as God sees you. Read the scriptures and have faith in the Most High God. It's no secret what the Lord can do. What he has done for others, he can do for you.

Lord Jesus, help me to see myself as You see me so I may fulfill Your purpose in my life. Thank You for Your presence that will always go with me. Amen!

Sausana Abraham

The Goodness of Jesus

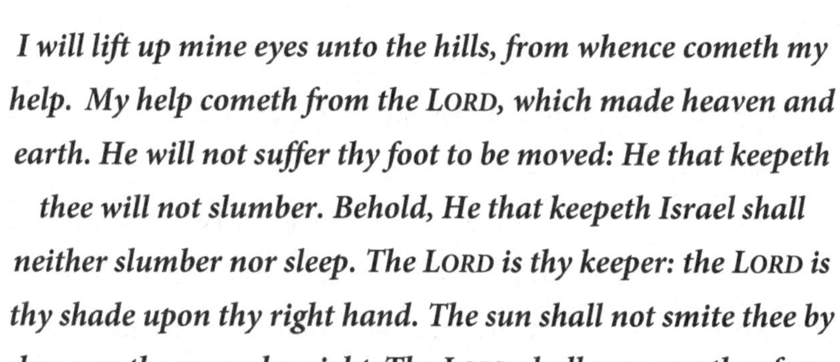

I will lift up mine eyes unto the hills, from whence cometh my help. My help cometh from the LORD, which made heaven and earth. He will not suffer thy foot to be moved: He that keepeth thee will not slumber. Behold, He that keepeth Israel shall neither slumber nor sleep. The LORD is thy keeper: the LORD is thy shade upon thy right hand. The sun shall not smite thee by day, nor the moon by night. The LORD shall preserve thee from all evil: He shall preserve thy soul. The LORD shall preserve thy going out and thy coming in from this time forth, and even forevermore. Psalm 121

As I traveled down the rugged pathway of life from day to day, I realized the many steep corners, high mountains, deep and dark valleys I encountered. I know I couldn't do it alone without the sheltering hands of Jesus reminding me that with Him and through Him I can make it.

When my husband died after ten (10) weeks of blissful pleasure, I found myself alone with a child on the way. It was very difficult but with good support from my family and strangers, I was able to smile again, having the full assurance that when we put our hands in the One who stills the raging seas, who comforts the widows and the fatherless, who heal the sick, feed the hungry and open doors that were closed. We can rejoice and rest assure that the God of Abraham, Moses, and Jacob who is our Deliverer will never leave nor forsake us (Heb. 13:5). This is a promise that is still binding today. We just must believe in Him.

Like the three Hebrew boys in the fiery furnace (Daniel 3:1-30) and Daniel in the lion's den (Daniel 6:1-28), they weren't afraid, so why should we. As (Isaiah 43: 1-3) states, Fear not for I will be with thee, when you pass through the waters it will not cover you, nor will you get burnt when you walk through the fire. For He is God.

My Jesus has seen me through all my dark days and is still doing so and He will do the same for you. Just trust Him and believe. I am rejoicing when I think of the goodness of Jesus and what He has done for me, my heart cries out Hallelujah, Thank God for saving me!

Gracious God, You know the desires of our heart. You know all that we stand in need of. And You know the burdens that grieve us. Help us Lord to lay every desire, need, and hurt at Your throne of grace and leave them there. Thank you, Father, Amen!

DNB

Faith

Honor the Lord with thy substance, and with the first fruits of all thine increase: so, shall thy barns be filled with plenty, and thy presses shall burst out with new wine. Proverbs 3:9,10

It was two weeks before the rent was due. My husband and I had just moved to Florida. We had enough money to purchase the necessary bedroom furniture and pay the first month's rent. The job my husband was working on with his dad was completed and I did not find a job yet. What were we going to do? We discussed the situation and went into praying for an entire week. At the end of the week, a family friend came by with good news giving me some information on a temporary caregiver assignment to begin the next morning. The job would be about 3-4 weeks.

Our God is an awesome God! The nursing facility where I had to go to work was within walking distance from our home. Every day I went to work and prayed that God would give me wisdom since this job was not something that I was used to. At the end of the week, my employer was quite pleased with my performance and I was given my wages. I put aside my tithe and when I counted the balance, there was enough to pay the rent the next day, with $4.00 left for groceries. I was grateful to God for providing this job and so on the following Sabbath, it gave me much happiness to put my tithe envelope in the offering plate, trusting God to see us through.

At the end of the next week, my employer said that she was taking her husband home and asked if I would come to her home to assist with him for a few weeks. I agreed, but now the prayer had to change, this time asking God to provide transportation because we did not own a vehicle. Again, I say...Our God is awesome. The bus that I needed to get to work came right down our street in front of our apartment building to turn around on its route. Hallelujah!

Being faithful to God has its blessings all the time. God will never turn back on His word. He has promised to "fill our mouth if we open it wide" (Ps. 81:10). I believe that because of God's faithfulness and my response to answered prayer, the job lasted for almost nine years. God provided every step of the way and we were never out of groceries. We always had enough and to share. The Lord promised to open the windows of heaven and pour us out a blessing. He sure did.

Heavenly Father, we thank you for Your faithfulness to us every day of our lives. Help us to determine in our hearts to be faithful to You, not just in tithe and offering, but in everything we do. We praise you in Jesus name. Amen.

Sharon Roberts

Trusting in God

Jesus said unto her, "I am the resurrection, and the life: he that believeth in me, though he were dead, yet shall he live" John 11:25

Father, thank you for opening the way for me to go to Uchee Pines Lifestyle Center. But Lord, you know I have been a picky eater all my life. Please, please don't let my cure be onions or anything slimy. I will eat everything else. Even... garlic. (And eat them I had to. Eight cloves, twice per day.) After being diagnosed with colon cancer, I was told I needed to have surgery. They would need to remove a sizeable mass. They said I would begin a course of chemotherapy, immediately following the operation. It was a grim picture. My entire life was turned upside down. But my sisters and I prayed for guidance, and it was then that we decided to give my body the opportunity to do what it was designed to do, heal itself. So, prior to undergoing natural therapy at Uchee Pines, my older sister enforced a radical diet change along with the use of various herbs and ALL the GREENS in the vegetable world. My pastor prayed with me and anointed me. A visiting pastor also anointed me. My church family prayed. My sister in France prayed along with her church there. And just before my journey to Alabama, some of my church sisters braided my hair.

June 3, 2018 - I had a four-hour layover in Atlanta. Time to think and pray. "I don't want to seem ungrateful God, but couldn't you have found another way to send me on vacation? Cancer God?" My answer to this question came instantly, softly, but clearly "That's the only way I could get your attention. You were too busy."

June 4, 2018 - Exhausted after an entire day of traveling. I arrived at Uchee Pines at midnight. Early the next morning there was orientation for the newly arrived patients. We were prayed with, fed, and then sent to bed.

June 5, 6, and 7 - Three days of fasting. We could only have herbal teas and water. I went for long walks every morning, only nature surrounding me. A group of us decided to revitalize the vegetable garden, in order to take our minds off food. We worked all three days, weeding, mulching, and transplanting. "Not by might nor by power but by My Spirit, says the Lord'. The vegetable garden was beautiful! It was filled with strawberries, vegetables, and flowers.

June 9, 2018 - Sabbath morning arrived, and we all set off for church on the campus. About half-way through the service, I began to feel some discomfort and pain in my stomach. The discomfort gradually increased. Not wanting to disturb the gathering, I tried stretching my legs under the pew in front of me, as far as they could reach. I was hoping for some relief. The medical team assigned to me somehow noticed that something was amiss and came over to enquire. They suggested leaving right away, but I opted to stay till the service ended. Then I was taken back to my room at the Lifestyle Center.

Back in my room the doctor examined me but could find nothing that would cause the pain. However, he decided to give me infrared treatment. He said, "Before you start the treatment, I will pray with you". I was sitting up in bed with my back against the headboard. My counselor sat directly in front of me, at the foot of the bed, while the doctor knelt beside me holding my hand. He began to pray. During the prayer, I had a very strong feeling that we had left the room and were in another place. So, convinced I was that I was no longer in the room I opened my eyes to see where we had gone. That is when I saw Him. Standing at the foot of my bed was a man clothed in a glowing robe of many colors, ivory, gold, blue, burgundy. The figure was very tall, and my eyes began traveling from the bottom of His robe, up and up until it reached just near the curve of his shoulders; where it appeared that clouds covered Him. I looked away and thought to myself. "Lord, with everything that is happening to me now, am I hallucinating?" I closed my eyes again and continued listening to the prayer. At the end of his prayer, the doctor said to me "Before you begin the treatment, I must tell you that while I was praying, I had the distinct impression that Jesus was in the room, standing right over there." He pointed to the place where I had seen the Person. I told the doctor what I had seen and how I had reacted. "Well,", he said "seems that this is confirmation for both of us!"

Dear Jesus, thank You for showing up when I needed You most. Thank You for Your presence throughout my treatments. Continue to increase my faith in You. In Jesus name Amen! - Aldyth Roach

Peace in the Midst of the Storm

Jesus was sleeping at the back of the boat with his head on a cushion. The disciples woke Him up, shouting, "Teacher, don't you care that we're going to drown?"
When Jesus woke up, He rebuked the wind and said to the waves, "Silence! Be still!" Suddenly the wind stopped, and there was a great calm. Mark 4: 38, 39 NLT.

When I was a little girl growing up in the Blue Mountain Hills of Jamaica, heavy winds and thunderstorms were common events, and still are. The most amazing and exciting thing for me was to watch the heavy dark clouds formed in the sky and across the mountainside. Next came light sprinkles of rain followed by torrential downpours. I would watch as trees swayed in the angry winds, the clear waters of the river gradually turned brown and spreads across the riverbed to the outer banks, fiercely swirling downwards gushing against boulders. As the thunders roared and lightning flashed across the sky, I ducked in fear as I huddled beside my mother.

As these events occurred more often, I questioned my parents about the person behind the storms and was told about God. I wanted to know more about this God who had these powers to activate the storms and stop them when He pleases.

I continued to question my parents but still did not get sufficient answers to quench my thirst. One day, a lady from the community stopped by our home selling children's books and my mother agreed for me to have a few of the Bible stories. As I read stories about creation, Noah and the Ark, Daniel in the lion's den to name just a few, my mind expanded, and I wanted to know more about this AMAZING God.

At the age of eight years old, I requested for my birthday, a Bible from my father, because I was now convinced that the answers to my questions lie therein. The more I read, the more I wanted to know, and be a follower of this God I was reading about. My heart rejoiced when at eleven years old I requested baptism and 44 years later I continue to walk with Him.

I've been through many storms in my life but the one constant that remained is that each time I was afraid, Jesus steps in, stretched out his strong arms, speaks to my problems, and says, " Peace be still."

Are there storms in your life? He can speak to them as He does to mine ...... if you ask Him to!

Dear God, I thank You for speaking to my storms each time they rage, and I'm tossed to and fro. Continue to walk with me as I trod this troubled world, and just in case the wind keeps blowing in my life, make Your presence known when I'm afraid and

think You're sleeping. Remind me Lord that my soul is anchored in YOU. Amen!!!

Georgia Douglas

Forgiveness

"If you forgive those who sin against you, your Heavenly Father will forgive you. But if you refuse to forgive others, your Father will not forgive your sins."

Matthew 6:14-15

Sometimes it's harder to forgive those we love the most and are closest to us. Yet it's through forgiveness that God heals us.

Growing up on the beautiful islands of the Bahamas wasn't as great and magnificent as it is for most children nowadays growing up. At ten years old I was raped by a family friend that left me traumatized up to this day. As a teenager, I started hanging out with the wrong crowd and acting as if I didn't care anymore because I felt as if my life wasn't my own. I eventually became sexually active and promiscuous with whomever I was dating at that time. I was then used and abused but at this point in my life, I didn't care because I felt no one else did.

I was in a 6-year relationship with my ex-boyfriend and things were going very well at first, but then old habits began, and things simply changed for the worse. I was beaten for breakfast, lunch, and dinner. You named it I was beaten for it. I was abused verbally, emotionally, and financially. I believed him every time he laid his hands on me and then apologized to me later. Repeatedly until it became a cycle of his. I thought that kind of treatment was love, I didn't know any better.

I started feeling guilty and tried ending my life several times because I felt as if nobody really cared for me at this point. One night after having enough of the abuse I prayed to God, "Father, bless me with the power of forgiveness, give me the grace to unconditionally forgive those who have done me wrong. You know my heart's desire; you know every detail of my life. Remove whatever bitterness may be in my heart, Lord, and fill the empty space with Your love. Amen"

At this point, I knew God was real and if I trusted in Him, He promised to be with me always.

The Bible says in Psalms 46:1 "God is our refuge and strength, an ever-present help in trouble." Let Him share your burdens and reveal His purpose for you.

I eventually left my ex-boyfriend and moved to another country. I forgave him for the way he treated me eventually because it says in the book of Colossians 3:13 "Make allowance for others faults and forgive anyone who offends you. Remember, the Lord forgave you, so you must forgive others.

Jesus, I know you love me. Please forgive me for my sins. Help me to be a better person. Amen.

Anonymous

Are You a Dreamer?

One day, Joseph told his brothers what he had dreamt, and they hated him even more."

Genesis 37: 5, CEV

Years ago, an African, Barack Hussein Obama, a Kenyan senior governmental economist, migrated to the United States of America to study. While there, he developed the passion and dream of becoming the first Black president, but he died without fulfilling that dream.

During the 1950s-60s, Martin Luther, Jr, a Baptist minister, and social rights activist in the United States of America had a dream of all African Americans having freedom, equal rights, and justice in a non-violent way. His greatest speech for this cause was the, "I have a dream" speech. However, he died without seeing the fulfillment of his dream.

In 2009, Barack Obama, became inspired and empowered by the vision and dreams of his father to become the first African American president. His campaign slogan, "Yes, We Can" ignited the hearts of people. This dream became a reality when he was elected as the 44th president. His inauguration was one of the largest ever to be watched by thousands of people all over the world.

In Genesis 37: 1-10, we read about Joseph, the dreamer who was sold into slavery by his brothers to prevent the fulfillment of his dream. In Egypt, he did not know what would happen, but God knew. Joseph endured twenty years of hardships in preparation to be a servant and leader in Pharaoh's palace. God's divine timetable for Joseph, the dreamer, was fulfilled when famine hit Canaan and his brothers had to travel to Egypt to buy grain.

Did you know that God had a dream for the whole world? In John 3: 16, the dream is revealed and today we can be a part of the fulfillment of this dream if we only believe and accept God's word. Jesus came he lived, suffered, died, was resurrected, and went back to heaven. His inauguration was watched by the heavenly host as God allowed Jesus to sit at His right hand on His throne where he is pleading on behalf of sinners.

Are you a dreamer? Have you been dreaming of Jesus' coming and the Holy City? In Revelation 21, John gave a vivid picture of the New Jerusalem, "There was no need of the sun ...moon to shine in it, for the glory of God did lighten it..."

Friends keep on dreaming, for if we faint not, one day soon this dream will be a reality, and not even death can prevent the faithful ones from living in this glorious city forever and ever.

Heavenly Father, we pray that whatever our dreams are, You will fulfill them according to Your will for our lives. Help us to trust in all circumstances. In Jesus' name. Amen.

Bula Haughton-Thompson

When All Else Fails

When I am afraid, I put my trust in you. Psalm 56:3 NIV

As I hustled to complete my chores, my hand brushed against my breast. What was that? Is that a lump I just felt? Was I mistaken? I immediately decided to examine my breast and without a doubt, there was, something there.

So, I made an appointment to see my OB/GYN and she confirmed that a lump was present. It was mental anguish! I was afraid of hearing the "C" word. Time seemed to have stopped. As I held back the tears, I listened as I was sent to have a biopsy. The results were uncertain, and I was told it would be best to remove the lump.

It was now time to pray earnestly and trust in God. You see, I had an aunt who died from breast cancer. I was afraid and I needed to trust in God. The surgery was scheduled, and I continued to pray asking God to spare my life for my two young children. I awoke to the surgeon presenting me with a photograph of the lump he had removed, as I had asked him to take a picture since I would not be conscious during the surgery. The lump was bigger than I thought. Seeing the picture brought home the realization of what was happening in my body. It was no longer just auditory. I now had a visual representation.

Now, I had to wait as the doctors checked for malignancy. Praise God! I received the news that it was benign. I praised God for His goodness. He had heard my cry and answered me. But this was only the beginning. Six months later, nearing Christmas, there was another lump. It has been about eight years now and the journey continues. Each year I continue to live with the uncertainty of not knowing if this is the year when I would be told its cancer. With each doctor's visit, my faith is strengthened.

I have been diagnosed with fibrocystic breast. My OB/GYN went as far as to tell me that I should donate my breast for research because I have what she called a textbook case of fibrocystic breast. So, every year I cross my finger and pray as I dutifully go for my OB/GYN visits, have my mammogram and sonogram. To date, I have had seven biopsies and two lumpectomies.

Talk about a life of trust! Each day I live with the uncertainty of not knowing if there will be another lump. I have undergone so many tests that I can longer keep track and it is difficult to recount and write my history each time I go for my mammogram.

Through it all, I have learned to trust in God. It has gotten to the point that when I go for my sonogram, I am now able to feel a sense of peace that I can fall asleep while being attended to.

Dear Jesus, I thank You for your continued care. I continue to place myself in your hands. For in your hands, I know I am safe. Please help me to always trust in you. In Jesus Name!

Michell Buttler

Trusting in God

It shall come to pass that before they call, I will answer and while they are still speaking, I will hear. Isaiah 65:24 (NKJV)

I was thrilled to receive a passing grade on the entrance exam. However, I did not have the required funds to begin classes the following week as I was informed. So now it's ...Prayer time! The next day, my day off, I received a casual call from a church member just to say hello and see what's new. I gave minimal information and ended the conversation after a couple of minutes.

About half an hour later while kneeling at my bedside talking to God about my need for funds to begin classes the next week, I heard a knock at the door and really was not happy that my prayer was being interrupted. When I opened the door, there was the same church member that I had just spoken to a few minutes ago, smiling and giving me an envelope saying something that sounded like "a gift from God", then left. I closed the door, opened the envelope, and praised the Lord loudly for a check of $100.

Later that night, another knock at the door. This time it was my husband's coworker bringing him a check for $100 which was money owed to him about six months ago. Did I mention how much was the registration fee to begin classes? Yes......$200. This time both my husband and I knelt and praised God for His faithfulness and for answered prayer.

God again reminded me that His promises are true, and I must trust Him at His Word. He also wants me to share these experiences and encourage others to cling to His promises.

Thank You, Heavenly Father, for Your faithfulness to us and for fulfilling Your promises in extraordinary ways. Help us to trust You completely and never doubt that You always want to do us good. We praise You for Your everlasting love, in Jesus' name. Amen!

Sharon Roberts

"Don't Worry"

"Therefore, I tell you, do not worry about your life, what you will eat or drink; or about your body, what you will wear. Is not life more than food, and the body more than clothes? Look at the birds of the air; they do not sow or reap or store away in barns, and yet your heavenly Father feeds them. Are you not much more valuable than they?" Matt. 6: 25-26

The truth is, we are surrounded by a mountain of fear, anxiety, and worry every day. We have no idea what will happen the next second, minute, hour, day, week, month, or year. How do I reopen my office? Should I cancel my dental appointment, should I go for my regular doctor's check-up, is it safe to go to church, should I go to visit a friend or a family member in the hospital, should I attend the funeral of a dear friend that succumbed to Covid19, should I worry about what my financial situation will be, and the list goes on. These are legitimate concerns about this pandemic. We have real struggles, real challenges, and real pain. Bad things happen to good people. Real problems do occur, usually daily. People don't act the way they ought to. Relationships falter and sometimes fail. There is chaos all around us. And there are certainly things that require concern and action on our part. So how do I maintain a calm demeanor and not worry?

Jesus knew this better than anyone. He spent most of his life being harassed and pursued by His enemies. So why did He tell us not to worry? Jesus knew that a life filled with fear has little room left for faith. And without faith, we can neither please God nor draw close to Him for the comfort and guidance we need to face the cares and affairs of everyday life. So, what is the difference between healthy concern and toxic worry? Here are a few things I've discovered in my own battle against fear:

Concern	Worry
Involves a legitimate threat	Is often unfounded
Is specific (one thing)	Is generalized (spreads to many things)
Address the problem	Obsesses the problem about the problem
Solves problems	Creates more problems
Looks to God for an answer	Looks to self or other people for answers

To sum it up, worry is allowing problems and distress to come between us and the heart of God. It is the view that God has somehow lost control of the situation and we cannot trust Him. A legitimate concern presses us closer to the heart of God and causes us to lean and trust in Him even more. *Concerns draw us to God... Worry pulls us from Him.*

So as your world seems to crumble around you, do not fear, do not worry; place your hand into the Hand of God. He can calm your fears, He can carry you through the darkest hours, He can lift you up through the deepest valley or the highest mountain. He can strengthen you, Yes, He will uphold you with His righteous right hand.

Dear Jesus in times when I want to worry, help me to remember to cast my cares on you because You care for me. Thank You for always being there to carry me through the roughest times of my life. Thank You for Your faithfulness towards me. In Jesus' Precious Name! Amen!

Dr. Donna Barrett

Forgiveness

"For I will be merciful to their unrighteousness, and their sins and their iniquities will I remember no more." Hebrews 8:12, KJV.

"Forgiveness is unlocking the door to set someone free and realizing you were the prisoner. "~Unknown. This was the quote that hit me head-on as I searched for where to start on forgiveness. It called me to pause and consider if this is truly how my spouse feels each time, he must alleviate my fears that he had yet to forgive me for something said in the heat of the moment. Did he really feel released when I pester him at every turn, whether he has honestly forgiven me for that thing that sometimes by that point neither of us remembered what it was?

A bigger question is, how does God feel when we keep bringing up the sin for which, we have already asked forgiveness for? Are we plaguing Him with a constant reminder of that thing that we claim that He has forgotten?

It, however, is not a mere claim but a promise. Isaiah 43:25; Jeremiah 31:34; Hebrews 8:12; and Hebrews 10:16-17 are just some of the texts from His words which, remind us that once He has forgiven our iniquities, He remembers them no more.

So, why are we not at peace with this? Do our doubts stem from our knowledge that God does not stay true to His word? I dare say that all of us would give a resounding "No" for an answer. Even the Bible would back us on that statement. "God is not a man, that He should lie..." Numbers 23:19, KJV. That will never change. Therefore, let us not lend our ears to the devil's whispers of trying to paint the Lord in a bad light but let us consciously hold onto His promise that He remembers our forgiven sins no more. Maybe it is high time that we forget them ourselves by never repeating them in words or by our deeds.

Dear Eloah Selikhot (God of Forgiveness/ Forgiving God), Help us to remember that when we come to you for true forgiveness that You are not only always quick to forgive but also to forget. Remind us through Your words when we are in doubt, but above all else, give us the strength to never walk that path of betrayal again. We thank You for Your merciful spirit, even when we sin against You. Give us the strength to overcome. In Jesus' name. Amen.

"For thou, Lord, art good, and ready to forgive; and plenteous in mercy unto all them that call upon thee." Psalm: 86:5, KJV.

Alex Thompson

Dealing With Tough Issues

For the spirit that God has given us does not make us timid; instead, His Spirit fills us with power, love, and self-control (2Timothy1:7, Today's English Version).

God has a purpose for each life. He made each of us in His image, to glorify His name and He will help us to fulfill His purpose, especially in tough times.

"I don't want to be a princess, I want to be a boy, like my brothers," five-year-old Jean yelled from her bedroom. Mother became curious and raced into Jean's bedroom, asking, "What's up with my little princess?"

"I tell you, I don't want to be a princess," Jean screamed. With tears rolling down her chocolate cheeks, she added, "I told you this before, but you won't listen."

"Okay, Baby. Mother is listening now."

"My brothers get to go outside and play basketball. They say I can't play; I should do girl's stuff. "Look at me," she continued through her sobs while tossing her dolls and tea set across the room. "Being a girl is boring!"

"But Jean, you do get to play basketball with your brothers, sometimes," the mother tried to encourage her daughter.

Hysterically she shouted, "No, no, I play only when they don't have friends. I want to play all the time. I don't want to be a girl!"

Mother held Jean closely to her, and trying to comfort her, she promised her that she will get to play with her brothers more often. With persistent prayers, intentional playtime with the brothers, daily pep talks, and close parenting, Jean got over the hurdle. She is now a beautiful, brilliant, young professional who is engaged to be married. God's plan for life is evolving day by day.

Today, more than ever, Christian parents are concerned about their children's feelings about their sexuality? When is the right time to talk to your children about gender differences and roles? How much should you say to your young children in order not to rob them of their innocence, nor to prejudice their thoughts about their sexuality? Our Creator cares about everything concerning our lives. God knew us before we were formed (Ps. 103:14), then we can trust Him to guide us and our children with their sexuality.

Lord, please help us to trust You in every aspect of our children's lives, including their sexuality. Amen!

Dr. Sandra Fletcher

Indescribable Peace

"Peace I leave with you, my peace I give unto you: not as the world giveth, give I unto you. Let not your heart be troubled, neither let it be afraid." John 14:27

Have you ever looked back at the way you handled a situation and wondered if that was you? Then you had to shake your head and say, "Thank you, Jesus! That had to be you!" I am so awed by the goodness of God! He truly is our Rock!

Some years ago, I had a problem with my right eye. It suddenly became very lazy on evenings, and I had to struggle to open it. I didn't think anything of it. I thought it was funny but was encouraged to get it checked out. My doctor sent me for a CT scan which showed either an expanding aneurysm or a tumor, and the next day, to my surprise, I was being flown to another country for further investigation and possible surgery. An MRI was done there, and it was determined that it was indeed a pituitary tumor, so that meant surgery. Neurosurgery.

I must stop here to explain something about myself. I am terrified of any invasive medical procedure, from injections upwards. Here I was, feeling very healthy, and within six days of my first visit to the doctor, I'm being prepped for brain surgery in another country. I should be panicking! I should be having anxiety attacks! I should be fearful and weepy! None of that was happening. A text that I had been teaching my class that week, John 14:27, is what kept coming back to me. It was as though my sweet Jesus had taken over and I was at peace! A peace that I couldn't understand!

This was 17 years ago, and I have regular consultations with the neurosurgeon. I will always remember the way Jesus put peace in my heart and carried me through what should have been the most difficult situation! I thank God for His love and mercy! He is awesome! His love and mercy are beyond our comprehension and I can say, with deep gratitude, "Thank you, Lord!"

Dear God, I thank You today and every day for how You care for me in the past and continue to care for me. I thank You for the peace that only You can give. I give You the praise that only you deserve. Help me to always trust in You. Amen!

Judith Alexander

God's Love

"All things were made by him, and without him was not anything made that was made." John 1:3, KJV.

Every day, we go to and fro, overlooking what we consider the little things. But sometimes, it is in those little things that we see God at His greatest. Today, as my husband drove me to work, I noticed a black Dodge zoomed by us before zigzagging through traffic and then disappeared ahead. After admiring the car while wondering where the driver had to go in such a hurry, I resumed my conversation with my partner. About a minute after, like deja vu, what seemed like the same car, did the same thing but this time overtaking on our left instead of the right. For a quick second, my brain wires fizzed, and I wondered if we were driving that slow for him to be able to be driving around us in circles. However, before I could start harassing my poor husband, my eyes caught the car's clock and speedometer. They both said otherwise. I was still going to ask him if he realized the car from earlier, but we drew upon a red traffic light. There sat the identical cars with almost identical license plate numbers- only a letter and a number different! I just burst out laughing-

much to his surprise- as I mentally nicknamed them the Dodge twins. I was just relieved that my pregnancy brain hadn't been playing tricks on me.

But it brought me squarely back to creation. Take the license plate of each car and externally you would be hard-pressed to find a difference. Job 12:7-10 says: "But ask now the beasts, and they shall teach thee; and the fowls of the air and they shall tell thee: 8. Or speak to the earth, and it shall teach thee: and the fishes of the sea shall declare unto thee. 9. Who knoweth not in all these that the hand of the LORD hath wrought this? 10. In whose hand is the soul of every living thing, and the breath of all mankind." (KJV). The Almighty God spoke, and it was so, yet we find uniqueness in each specimen. More so with mankind. The Great I Am could've muttered and called man forth but with great love and tenderness, He got down into the dust and molded us into His image, each with his own unique characteristics. Even identical twins have different fingerprints. Isn't that amazing? His love goes beyond our finite understanding!

Heavenly Father, cause us to see that no matter how similar we may seem to be with our parents, siblings, family members, or even strangers that we are still unique in your loving eyes. You will never mistake us for another, even though millions of us call upon You at the same time. Let us continue to use this uniqueness to glorify You. In Jesus' name. Amen!

"Hearken unto this, O Job: stand still, and consider the wondrous works of God." Job 37:14, KJV.

Alex Thompson

Angels Take Care of Us

"The angel of the LORD encampeth round about them that fear him, and delivereth them." Psalms 34:7 (KJV)

There are texts in the Bible that we learn as children growing up in various churches. We memorized texts about the love of God, the Word of God, the Ten Commandments, and angels. One of the texts that I remember as a child is our text for today about angels delivering people. But are angels real? Can we see them? How can we be sure that they exist? And what is their real purpose here on earth?

Back in the islands some years ago, my husband and I were traveling back home late one Sunday evening. About half the way home we had to drive through a few miles of lonely roads with no houses. It was a little before sunset so we would have enough time to get home just before dark. Suddenly we heard a familiar but unwelcome noise, and the car began to bump. Yes, we had a flat tire. My husband quickly pulled to the side of the road and popped open the trunk of the car to retrieve the jack and change the tire. As I was getting out of the car, I heard him say with a loud groan, "oh nooo". Someone had borrowed the jack and did not return it.

Now, what were we going to do? At this time on a Sunday evening, there's no hope of seeing any frequent traffic on this road. I cannot remember who prayed but suddenly, we saw a huge black truck coming our way. The truck pulled over to the side of the road in front of us and the driver walked back to see what was wrong. After speaking with my husband, he went back to the truck and returned with a jack and gave it to my husband saying, "I have to go but you can give it to me when you see me". And with that, he turned around, got back in his truck, and drove away just as mysteriously as he came.

When we see you? Who are you? We never saw you before, and if we see you again who says we will remember who you are? My husband changed the tire as fast as he could, and we hurried on home spellbound as to what just happened.

Later that night we talked about the incident before going to bed and thanked God for His providence. However, to this day I am convinced that the truck driver was an angel sent from God to help us, and I won't be surprised when I get to heaven if I see this man walk up to me and say, "remember me?" And in his hand, he will be holding a golden jack.

Father, we thank You for loving us so much that You sent Your angels every day and night back and forth from Heaven to earth to take care of us and protect us from harm and danger. Amen!

Sharon Roberts

Jesus our Guiding Light - Sunrise Encounter

But now is Christ risen from the dead, and become the first fruits of them that slept 1 Corinthians 15:20(KJV)

My husband and I took a relaxing walk by the seaside across from our house. Just one stare of the shimmering, clear water was sufficient to entice me to step in though not planned. Gleefully, I stepped right in and then contemplated remaining right there because of the calming effects the warm water had on me. Here is where the abundant scented seaweeds and the varied shapes and sizes of the rocks infused my lungs and massaged my feet, giving much relief and renewed energy at the end of a hectic day.

After a peaceful night, I was awakened at the crack of dawn to sounds of the cock-a-doodle-do, cluck, cluck and peep, peep, peep of the roosters, hens, and their chicks. Reaching for my devotional box, I sprung out of bed and went out on the verandah to enjoy the tranquility of early hours and meditate on

God's mercy and goodness. Sitting there, the silence became deafening as I couldn't hear a stir or sound of anything man-made. Instead, the sun was the only thing that moved out of its dwelling slowly rising to color the horizon in crimson, orange. Its glimmer through my coconut and bougainvillea wrapped casuarina trees created a spectacular and glorious picture. Amazingly, it began occupying the streets and land as if to say this is all my residence for the day.

This early morning scene of the rising sun forced me into a reflection of the Rising Son of Righteousness on that early Easter Sunday morning. I wondered if it was a morning like this when Christ our Savior rose. My admiration of the beauty created by the sun shifted my thoughts to the incredible hope, joy, and beauty the rising sun and the Son of God brought to us as they rose together that Sunday morning. The hope that I will rise to meet Him when He returns just as He rose when He left to prepare that place for us in His Father's kingdom.

Our Heavenly Father, thank You for the sacrifice You made so we can find salvation full and free. We place all our hope in You today. As we look forward to Your return, help us to be ready, and to prepare others for Your kingdom in your precious Son's name. Amen!

Carol Nyack nee Gopaul

Strength Through His Word

God is a refuge and strength a very present help in trouble. Therefore, will not fear, even though the earth be removed, and though the mountains be carried into the midst of the sea (Psalm 46:1-2).

God's word has been an integral part of my life from a little girl. My parents made sure we had morning and evening worship every day. My sibling and I were taught that the word of God is a lamp unto our feet and a light unto our path. My parents were committed to teaching us about the love of God through His words.

We made it a habit to study our memory verses each week. Each Sabbath morning, we repeated Scriptures from memory. At the end of each quarter, my siblings and I recited 13 scriptures from memory. We were all happy to memorize and took pride in our presentation.

As an adult, I have made reading the Word an integral part of my life. Without it, I'm not sure where I would be. It is a wonderful feeling when you can read, understand, comprehend, and memorize the Word. In my quiet moments, I read the word and am encouraged by His promises.

As I reflect on my life, and how far the Lord has brought me, I can't help but praise and magnify Him. I sincerely thank Him for His Word that brings me strength when I am weak, courage when I am fearful, comfort when I am grieving, and hope when I am lost.

Hebrews 4:12 (NKJV) "For the Word of God is living and powerful, and sharper than any two-edged sword, piercing even to the division of soul and spirit, and joints and marrow, and is a discerner of the thoughts and intents of the heart.

"Run to Him, lay down your weapons, and fall into His arms. Acknowledge that He is God and that He is exalted in the earth. So as your world crumbles around you, the call from Scripture is, "don't flinch in faith in God. Stand still—not because of a self-made confidence, not because you are the most composed person in the face of disaster, not because "you've seen it all." But because God is in charge.

Eternal Father, we are thankful for Your word. Your word is a lamp unto our feet and a light to our path. We could not live without the assurance and the blessed hope in Your word. Continue to bless and keep us as we make Your word a part of our life each day. Amen.

Dr. Donna Barrett

His Love

Then Peter came to Jesus and asked, "Lord, how many times shall I forgive my brother or sister who sins against me? Up to seven times?" Jesus answered, "I tell you, not seven times, but seventy-seven times. {Matthew 18:21-22 NIV}

Our friendship happened so fast. We went from strangers one day to best friends the next. She became my confidant. But as my mother always said, *"for every best friend that friend has a better friend, and often that isn't you."*

When the friendship between two people comes to an impasse one often is left confused and constantly wonders what the cause is. It gets worse if only one is being open and upfront with their feelings. Jesus also had this experience. The only difference is that He wasn't confused with the intentions of His friend. However even amidst the build-up of the deception by Judas, Jesus' love for him never changed but remained constant.

The story of Judas's deception leading up to the death of Jesus is so amazing. When we take into consideration the tender care in the heart of Jesus displayed to the very ones who hated him, and to the disciple that betrayed Him, we notice that His love for mankind didn't change at any given moment.

In life, we may often realize that the most painful betrayals come from those who are closest to us, yet despite our feelings of betrayal God will teach us how to forgive if we are willing to do so. At some point in our lives, we will experience betrayal and the hurtful feeling that accompanies it, whether we are the giver of the act or not, yet when we take notice of Jesus and dare ourselves to respond like him, we will realize that nothing can separate us from the love of God. Our Christian duty is to allow the love of Jesus to flow through us and we will learn that although our trust may be broken, we can lean on the very one that understands all our emotions. He can walk us through the pain and hurt we may feel and show us how to be loved, give love and forgive through it all.

Dear Lord, according to Your word you are a father who understands everything we go through and You tell us whenever we are in need, we should come boldly before Your throne. Right now, I am feeling betrayed, and it hurts. My heart hurts but I am thankful that I can find comfort in knowing that You understand, and You can and will see me through. Father, despite the hurt that I feel, I ask you to help me to pray my friendships back to life. Amen!

Kaye Ann Clarke

Trusting God

Proverbs 3 vs 5-6: Trust in the LORD with all your heart and lean not on your own understanding; in all your ways submit to him, and he will make your paths straight. "Trust God, Leave the Consequences to Him"

"You did not pass the test." I stood completely still as the ground seemed to move beneath me. I could not believe it! I had studied for weeks and invested $200 in taking this test, and just like that, the certificate was gone. It was my last shot at being hired as a teacher. "You won't be able to retake it for another 30 days and it will be another $200." I thanked the gentleman and took my exit. Lord, how could you let me fail that test, you know I needed it. "Just trust me, Terry," Those words can be honey and acid all at the same time, but I had no choice. I decided to trust Him.

With schools opening in a week, I pursued God about what to do next. I clearly heard the Lord tell me to apply for teaching positions. Without my certificate? Lord are you sure? Once He confirmed His word, I moved forward with applying. I was elated when it took less than 24 hours for me to hear from two schools.

Now I wished I had some perfect Job story to share, but my faith wavered immensely. I was very doubtful that a principal would hire me without the necessary certificate. This first interview was an absolute nightmare, and my Spirit was crushed. "God, what are you doing?" "This makes no sense!" "Trust me, Terry." This time God's reassuring words were pure acid. I wanted to know what God was up to and it frustrated me. But I decided to put Daniel's God to the test one more time. I would trust Him and leave the consequences to Him.

The second interview came. After a few questions, the principal donned a huge smile and said, "You are perfect for the Job! I will give you a month to retake your test, but you are hired!" Let me tell you about Daniel's God! He will deliver! Psalm 20:7 says, *some nations boast of their chariots and horses, but we boast in the name of the Lord our God.*

God never makes a promise He does not intend to keep. Trust in Him and leave all the consequences to Him.

Lord thank You that You are faithful to the end. There is no God who is like You! Please help me to trust You even if the situation seems hopeless. Even when it makes absolutely no sense, please Lord help me to put my confidence in You. You are faithful and You keep Your promises. Amen!

Terry-Ann Talbert

Trusting in God

"Though he slays me, yet will I trust him" Job 13:15

We sometimes face circumstances, which are sudden, unexpected, and with negative or even life-changing impacts. We may feel confused, embarrassed, and undeserving of our situation. What should we do when our lives have been turned upside down and our future seem uncertain? TRUST GOD!

I have pursued a healthy lifestyle since my youth and was illness free up to the age of 72.

I looked, felt better, and was more active than would be expected from someone of my age. I suddenly developed an illness, which left me with serious symptoms including blindness. Though surprised and confused by my illness, I was grateful that I did not react negatively. Instead, I experienced a feeling of peace and acceptance, which I knew was a gift from God. That reinforced my decision to continue to trust Him.

Job is an example of someone with great trust in God. It is worth reading his experience in the Bible. After losing his children, servants, wealth, and possessions, and experiencing an attack on his body causing painful sores, he concluded that even if God killed him, he would continue to trust Him (Job 13:15). That kind of trust develops from a close relationship with God.

A close relationship with God can be developed by: *1) Thinking about* what our loving God has done for us. For example, He created a beautiful world for us, and though marred by sin and human action there are still many beautiful parts of our world. He saved us from eternal death through the sacrifice of Jesus (John 3:16). He gave us life and has cared for us from birth to the present. He has provided us with food, shelter, protection, and guidance. Even if we face challenges such as abuse, neglect, and oppression, the fact that we are alive and have hope for the future is evidence of God's mercy and faithfulness towards us (Lam 3:22-25). *2) An active prayer life.* Speaking to God as to a friend, we can share with Him our joys, sorrows, and challenges, and seek His assistance in guiding our lives. *3) Studying the word of God.* This teaches us about the character of God and guides us in how we should live, and how we should relate to God and those around us.

As for me, my overall condition is improving, and I am more optimistic about the future. I do not expect to regain my sight except God intervenes miraculously. I, my family and friends are praying for such a miracle. However, I will continue to trust Him even if my sight is not restored, confident that he will act in my best interest. I, therefore, encourage us all to trust God in all circumstances.

Heavenly Father, amid our challenges, confusion, and despair, may we learn to trust You in all circumstances of life. Amen!

Silvia Ham-Ying

Hope

"For I know the plans I have for you," declares the LORD, "plans to prosper you and not to harm you, plans to give you HOPE and a future. Jer. 29:11

As a child, I'd often heard my grand and great grandparents quote these scriptures: such as Hebrews 11:1, "Now faith is the substance of things hoped for, the evidence of things not seen", and 1 Corinthians 15:19 "If in this life only we have hope in Christ, we are of all men most miserable." At first, I didn't understand what these scriptures meant. But as I grow older, these scriptures became more relevant and significant to me and even took precedence in my life.

I had many things I was hoping to accomplish, such as becoming a doctor, getting married, having a home of my own, etc. But I never knew it would have taken such great faith to accomplish these things that I was hoping for. You see, my mother had nine children, I was the third of the nine. The two oldest weren't living at home, so I became the eldest. This meant most of the responsibilities of the home were placed on me. My mother had to work hard to support us. There was not much help or no help at all from the fathers of us all. I didn't get the chance to attend school as other children did. My hope of becoming a doctor seemed out of my reach.

At the age of twelve years old, I became very depressed. Obtaining an education was not in my favor and I had no control over this. I rebelled about everything and asked my mother to send me to live with my dad. I was hoping, then, that things would be better, and it was, for just a single year. I was enrolled in school, but I struggled with reading and math, but I was determined to learn and become a doctor.

I was a child who had no control over my own life and no one to help me. At the hands of my father, I endure incestual, physical, emotional, psychological, and financial abuse, like no other child had ever experienced. This pattern followed me into adulthood. Every person I encountered found a way to take advantage of me one way or another. All my hopes, of becoming anything worth meaningful or accomplishing anything for myself were smashed into pieces.

Just when I thought to myself, all hope was gone, I met Jesus, and praise God, Jesus has changed my entire life. He has given me not only hope, but also a future. I went to Northern Caribbean University and studied nursing. I migrated and is now continuing with my studies. I still have that hope of becoming a doctor. I will not give up, because all my hope is in Jesus.

What are you hoping for today, my friend? I give you Jesus. He will make it possible for you. Won't you accept him today? Let Him change your life and give you the direction you are hoping for.

Dear Jesus, thank you for showing up in my circumstances. I praise You for Your faithfulness. Amen!

Marcia Scott

Thanksgiving

O the depth of the riches both of the wisdom and knowledge of God! How unsearchable are His judgments, and His ways past finding out! Romans 11:33

As I sit, contemplating life, I think of how often a "Thanks!" "I appreciate that." "Thank you!" or "Thank God" has entered my ears or exited my lips. Most times I've heard or uttered those words, they were in reaction to something received. Whether it is a door held open for the next person, a kind deed was done in a time of need, or an unexpected material gift, it is and has been customary to say thank you. As I think more deeply, I realize how easy it is to be thankful when something positive happens. At times, those two words bounce off our lips almost reflexively. What about when things aren't so positive?

It can be difficult to thank God when your car won't start, and you need to be at an important appointment in a few minutes. It can be even harder when you get some unfavorable news from your doctor. Still, harder is it to give thanks, when your loved one has passed away. Not everything that happens to us as children of God brings beaming smiles. How, then, does the Bible instruct us to give thanks in everything (1 Thess. 5:18)?

The answer is trust in God. This fuels true thankfulness. According to Romans 11:33, His judgments and ways are unsearchable, and His wisdom unfathomable. He is not sleeping when positive or negative things occur in our lives. He allows them all for His purpose. Instead of losing hope in those negative examples above, trust in God will allow you to thank Him for saving you from a possible accident you would have been in had your car been working; for His healing according to His will or life transformation of someone else through your trial; or even for all the years you had to enjoy that loved one before they passed. Trust in God causes the words "thank you" to bounce off our lips as easily in bad times as in good times.

Lord, thank You for your wisdom and care. Help me to give thanks in all things, because You know what's best. In Jesus' name, Amen!

Iska Stoddart

Hope

Now, Faith is the substance of things hoped for the evidence of things not seen. Hebrew 11:1.

When we are faced with a now situation, we need a Now Faith to pull us out and this is not an easy thing to do. We know that God is an ever-present help in the time of trouble, yet we panic we give into frustration we let fear take over. When trouble, sickness, financial difficulties, etc. comes our way we are to hold fast to our faith in God. For God is faithful, He that promise. Now Faith means at that very same time as you're praying you must see the answer which is the thing that you are hoping or praying for in your mind's eyes you must VISION the answer as if it is already received, when you do this, it becomes the evidence of things hoped or prayed for. When you have evidence, you have proof means it is shown and to be shown it is present.

I was twenty-three (23) weeks pregnant when I went to the hospital to get a scan. Upon getting the scan I was rushed into the maternity ward. I was told I had no water, my baby was in the vaginal walls, and that I was having a miscarriage. I was told by my doctor that the hospital will only try and save a 24-week baby and my baby is 23 weeks old. Through a prophet and through the word God, I was told that I was carrying a prophet so my faith kicked in. I said to myself, a prophet and a miscarriage don't add up. I'm not having a miscarriage, my baby shall live and not die. I told the doctor if he needed one more week, I will stay in the hospital, but my baby will live. My son was born on the day that made the 24 weeks. He came out kicking, although he only weighed one pound. John had many challenges, but everything the doctor said would go wrong because of my age at that time didn't. John was born on October 2nd. I was 47 years old. He is now 11 years old and have never been back in the hospital. FAITH WORKS!

Dear Heavenly Father I receive the answer to my prayer by faith, knowing that it is already done, for Your word says when I pray whatever I ask for in Jesus name believe I receive and I will have it, so thank You father for ever-increasing Faith in Jesus'

name I pray. Amen!

Gwen Greenslade

The Holy Spirit

"But now I am going away to the one who sent me, and not one of you is asking where I am going. Instead, you grieve because of what I've told you. But in fact, it is best for you that I go away because if I don't, the Advocate won't come. If I do go away, then I will send him to you. John 16:5-7

Watching someone you love leaving is one of the hardest things to experience, you start to think of all the things you'll miss, the memories you won't be part of, and the important lessons you could've to learn from them. If I was to guess, that's probably what was going through the mind of the disciples. Reminiscing of everything they've been through with Jesus, from healing the sick, watching him cast out demons, and helping him feed the crowd. Nonetheless, they are now faced with a new reality, a journey without the son of God. Despite what they felt inside, Jesus knew the importance of why he had to leave, there's more work to be done.

The Holy Spirit is here to continue the work of the gospel, and he does it by transforming your life into the likeness of Jesus

Christ. As you continued in this journey of growing in Christ, you might feel saddened at times just as the disciples felt in the beginning, but take heart beloved, for you are not alone, you have a helper, a comforter, and an advocate. From this day forward, I invite you to continue in the hope we have in Jesus Christ by believing in what the scriptures say in John 14: 3-4 "When everything is ready, I will come and get you, so that you will always be with me where I am. And you know the way to where I am going."

Father in Heaven Lord, I thank You for Your grace and mercy. I know I am not worthy of Your favor in my life, but You have chosen me to be set apart for Your glory. Please help me to surrender to You and to trust the work the Holy Spirit is doing in my life. I pray that He will continue to guide me and help me to live a life pleasing to You, change my desire Lord, give me a right spirit and a new heart. I pray and believe I will be who You have called me to be, a daughter. Let the words of my mouth and the meditation of my heart be acceptable in Your sight. In Jesus' name, I pray, Amen!

Lookha Albert

The Price of Twenty Twenty

Understand this, my dear brothers and sisters. You must all be quick to listen, slow to speak, and slow to get angry. James 1:9

Opening that letter on Sabbath morning brought tears to my eyes. How is it that no one even asked me for an explanation concerning the matter before the verdict was unanimously made? This was the first thought that came to my mind as I read the decision that was made based on the allegations. However, I was guilty of the accusation so now it was time to deal with the consequences of my actions. I felt like an injustice was being done in the matter plus the stipulations of the punishment were unjustified in my opinion. No one understood how and why the incident happened, no one even bothered to ask, and now this?

Pride truly goeth before a fall, your head swells and you justify that you must defend the issue for yourself because only you can handle it in the way it needs to be dealt with - even if in your defense your brother or sister gets hurt. I was in that moment, surrounded by friends, and I couldn't care less how my actions had caused another to stumble in her words and thoughts, if I got my deed done. Funny thing though I was always aware that the way I dealt with certain situations often was tactless but that didn't bother me. What mattered was that you knew how I felt that I was right, and you were wrong. However, we serve a God who use ways only He can to highlight the rot within us, not to hurt us but to grow, transform, and fit us for heaven. It took a time out from God, not from our connectedness, but from the things that distract such as church office and positions to show me that I sure can't march to Zion trampling on others. Like a caring Father God taught me the right way to deal with others; not to always be the one who thinks that I know everything but in love, pick and choose battles, and even often bridling my unruly tongue because not everything deserves a lashing answer. To hold pride dearly hurts but it can cost even more too. It can cost us eternal life.

Lord may the lessons and the bitter hurt of pride not be found in me when You come. Please do a cleansing within me through the abiding presence of Your Holy Spirit, so that I may not be a stumbling block unto others. Amen

Kaye Ann Clarke

Thanksgiving

Enter into his gates with thanksgiving, and into his courts with praise: Be thankful unto Him and bless his name. Psalm 100:4

Thanksgiving is my recognition of the many blessings, protections, and spiritual discernment that God has provided me throughout my life. First, as Creator of the universe who made the heavens, the sun, moon, stars, and galaxies. In his omniscient power, he installed the plan of salvation for a sinner like me, even before I was thought of or ever to be born. There are no words to describe his magnificence, but to be grateful and thankful for all that he has done and is still doing. This my Thanksgiving Prayer.

Thank you, Lord, for placing me as a babe in my mother's arms for taking care of me and soothing her nightly fretful qualms. Thank you, Lord, for taking care of every little thing even when living on a budget was meager like a shoestring. You provided my daily sustenance as nourishment, for my weary broken body to keep on living, and for this, I know, there is no end to your giving.

Thank you, Lord, for upholding me in times of doubt, for reminding me to reflect on times past,

and give you praise with a tremendous shout. Thank you, Lord, for the opportunity to achieve an education. In giving me the ability to put pen to paper and write without hesitation. Thank you, Lord, for family, friends, and mentors who were a positive influence, a source of strength and encouragement. In my moments of despair, for persistently reminding me, that God is always with me and loves me with the utmost tenderest care.

Thank you, Lord, for the recognition that there is no mountain too high, no valley too low, or ocean too wide, where your presence cannot be felt. When I think about these things, in deep contrition my heart just melts.

What a good God you are, what a mighty God you are, what a bulwark and force you are to be reckoned with. Who is like unto you? None other in the heavens nor on earth. You never left me, you have always been there for me, which has reinforced in my mind the reason for your death on calvary's tree, the plan of salvation which is free; to save a sin-sick nation and rescue a dying soul like me.

This is my Thanksgiving Prayer and praise God from whom All blessings flow. Amen!

Faith D. Housen

I Am Forgiven

"For if I forgive other people when they sin against me, My Heavenly Father will also forgive me." Matthew 6:14.

The prophet promotes a gift from God, which is forgiveness and mercy. Such beautiful gift is a promise from our Heavenly Father. God's mercy shows up in our lives at salvation (Titus 3:5), and He continually and daily shows us mercy in forgiveness (1 John 1:9). He extended mercy in shielding Israel, sending prophets to warn them of sin and draw them back to Himself. God saved us, not because of righteous works, but according to his own mercy, by the washing of regeneration and renewal of the Holy Spirit, Colossians 3:13.

But when the goodness and loving kindness of God our Savior appeared, He saved us, not because of our works in righteousness, but according to His own mercy; by the washing of regeneration and renewal of the Holy Spirit, whom He poured out on us richly through Jesus Christ our Savior; so that being justified by His grace we might become heirs according to the hope of Eternal Life. In Psalm 130; 3,4: God has not dealt with us according to our sins, nor punished us according to our own iniquities. For as the heavens are high above the earth, so great is His mercy toward those who fear Him; as far as the East is from the West, so far, He has removed our transgressions from us.

Then I shall not be ashamed when I have respect unto all thy commandments. Wherewithal shall a young man cleanse his way. By taking heed thereto according to thy word. With my whole heart have I sought thee: O let me not wander from thy wander from thy commandments. Psalm 119: 8-10

Heavenly Father, thank You for Your forgiveness. Thank You for Your grace and loving-kindness. Keep us firmly in our trust in You our hope through the comfort which is in You. We love You and honor You in Jesus' Holy name Amen!

Dr. Maryse Desir

Trusting In God

Trust in the Lord with your all heart, and do not lean on your own understanding. Proverbs 3:5

Trusting in God is always how I went about life. I experienced so much at a young age; all I can do is just cry out to him. I experienced teenage motherhood at 15 years old. I experienced losing my Father at 24, my Mother at 25, My grandmother at 26, and my daughter's Aunt at 27. Four years of loss and could still barely mourn the loss of my mother, my best friend. There were times I had to sit and think why all this is happening. I had to learn to trust God in his journey at the time, it was yet difficult, but I had to trust Him.

As the years went by, I realized that all that I experienced made me stronger in areas that I needed to focus more on God. I was not having an intimate relationship with Him during those years. At that time, it was hard to grasp, but it brought me so much closer to Him. Sometimes the pain we endure in life allows us to open more to God and trust in Him in all the decisions He has for our life.

Having an intimate relationship with God has allowed me to be transparent, strong, determined to live by His will, and learn to accept what He has in store for me. Psalm 28:7 The Lord is my strength and my shield, in him my heart trust, and I am helped: my heart exults, and with my song, I give thanks to him. God had a plan for me. That plan was here before I journeyed here on earth. That plan included having a child at a young age and losing my parents at a young age. These experiences have allowed me to trust Him and grow stronger in my relationship with Him. God knows all and seeks for us to put Him first above all things and trust in Him.

Father God, I thank You for humbling me and allowing me to always trust in You even when there were times that I cannot forsake what You have planned for me. Father God thank You for always allowing me to trust in You even when times seemed as if I could not get by or understood where I was going. Thank You, God for always protecting me and my family and allowing me to be transparent with you even in times of where I find myself lacking faith.

Leteshia Lewis

Radical Faith

Rahab knew that the only way she could obtain protection from destruction was to risk everything she had. In order to have faith in God, she had to lose faith in everything else! Faith is believing in someone or something you can't see. (Heb. 11:1). Rahab could have turned the spies in and then benefited from the reward of being the one who captured them. She could have discounted the many stories she heard about the Israelites and their God. But Rahab based her faith not on who she is; a woman of Jericho, a prostitute, a woman living on the outside of the city walls, but Rahab based her faith on who God is - the God who does what He says He will do, who keeps His promises, and who protects and saves His people. And in doing so, Rahab willingly surrendered everything she had to His mercy!

Are you going to say, "I AM FAITHFUL," "even though I don't know what the test result will be, I AM FAITHFUL" Even though I did not get that job, I AM FAITHFUL, even though I don't know how I am going to pay my bills, I AM FAITHFUL because I know God's got my back, I AM FAITHFUL!

Rahab's faith was honored so much later in the New Testament – for this is the kind of faith that moves the heart of God. When a person surrenders everything, places everything they know, love, and trust on the line and at the mercy of God. Then God marvels at and rewards their faith. This is the kind of faith that can move mountains. That is Radical Faith.

The kind of faith that Rahab had is the kind of faith that gives rise to hope no matter what circumstance you find yourself in. It is the kind of faith that lifts you up and carries you through the darkest and bleakest times. For, it is during those times that it isn't always easy to see the light, feel the love, or hear the voice of God! But that doesn't mean that He isn't there!!!

Despite the challenges, I AM FAITHFUL that God is going to come through. My faithfulness is based on His ever-present help in my past experiences. Yes, I AM FAITHFUL!!!

Our God and Father, thank You for this excellent example of radical faith. Help me to develop faith, even as small as a mustard seed. Help me to remain faithful even though it appears that there is no light at the end of the tunnel. Enrich me with Your grace. Increase my faith. Amen!

Dr. Donna Barrett

Faith

"But without faith, it is impossible to please him, for he that cometh to God must believe that he is a rewarder of them that diligently seek him." Hebrew 11:6

To have faith in God is to be grounded, secure, and unmovable Like a mountain. It is the unfettering belief that as the four seasons in nature follow a cycle without fail, which was created by the God of the universe. Faith is to know as night follows day, the sun will shine after the rain, but most of all faith is to know that God is a God of the impossible. Man's disappointment in life is God's opportunity to act on his behalf through faith. Remember Paul said in Hebrews 11:1 "Faith is the substance of things hoped for the evidence of things not seen."

Fearful, doubtful, and troubled. I was facing one of my darkest days. The old feelings of failure crept into my mind, anxious thoughts pervaded my head, and I could steadily feel my blood pressure rising. Another sleepless night lay ahead, what could I do? I was in my bedroom when I heard the birds outside the window frantically trilling loudly. I thought to myself, how did they know to come to my bedroom window, they are usually by the kitchen window near the back door. I got up, peeked through the window, then went to the back door. The birds came flying by, lined up on the fence and in the tree crying for food. The spot where I normally would feed them was empty. I went inside, got their food, and fed them. I watched them as they flew down with confidence to eat their food. I studied them as they shared the food without fighting. I listened to them as they softly cooed, as a melodious trill emanated from their voices. They were calm and peaceful, now that their immediate need for hunger had been met.

I said to myself God you are so good, your word never fails. Your eyes are on the sparrow and I know you will watch over me. I know If you can feed these birds, you will feed and take care of me. I had lost my job and I didn't know how I was going to pay the mortgage plus other bills. I was alone in a new state and had the responsibility of taking care of my elderly mother. I cried out to God and begged him to give me the faith to believe in Him and not give up. I asked him to quell my fears and dark thoughts. I asked him for inner peace and deliverance from all evil. I just kept repeating the words *"God if you can take care of the birds, you will take care of me and my mother."* Just give me the faith to believe. In his own time God answered my prayers. He found another job for me and much closer to home. He paid my bills for me, he used human vessels to support me in my time of need. I was not made homeless, and he took care of my aging mother.

Dear God thank You for giving me this thought of encouragement, to share my faith to help others who may be facing similar situations. I thank You for your mercy and grace to the open line of the royal, the twenty-four-hour connection, which is never busy. Thank You for teaching me that faith is the victory that overcomes the world. – Faith Housen

Watch Your Words

A word fitly spoken is like apples of gold in pitchers of silver
Proverbs 25:11

The language that we use to communicate has meaning. Human beings use written or spoken words to express themselves. Hence, the speaker and the audience. The words that we speak can carry different messages depending on the speaker, the audience, and their backgrounds. Some words are uplifting and cause the listener to feel good and other words are meant to demean or to hurt. How can the same mouth speak good and bad words?

The Bible says: Out of the abundance of the heart, the mouth speaks. This suggests that there is a thought process going on in one's mind before he or she utters a word. Proverbs 25:11 states, A word fitly spoken is like apples of gold in pitchers of silver. Think about it, as flowery a language as it seems, apples of gold and pitchers of silver connotes something pleasing to the eye and is uplifting to the spirit. It makes you feel good inside.

Hence, when you speak well of each other or encourage with kind words, it makes you feel good.

The Psalmist David said in Psalm 119: 105: Thy word is a lamp unto my feet and a light unto my path. He is speaking about God and his character. God. If our heavenly Father is mindful of his words, so should we, His children. No wonder David is described as a man after God's own heart. David sang praises and danced before the Lord (2 Samuel 6:14).

Speak kind words, encourage others to do good, and wish them well. Build up and not destroy.

Christians have an awesome task to do. Not only do they have to carry their own burdens, but they need to help others as well. The young people look to adults for guidance and nurturing. Adults need to be careful about how they speak to young ones. Weigh your words carefully before you speak them because words can kill or destroy.

Hebrews 4:12 said, for the word of God is quick and powerful, sharper than any two-edged sword, piercing even the dividing asunder of soul and spirit, and of the joints and marrow, and is a discerner of the thoughts and intents of the heart. This puts God's thoughts high above ours. Moreover, He knows the intents of our hearts. Therefore, it makes good sense to weigh our words before we speak them. Speak good words and do kind deeds. Brothers and sisters, "let us love one another, for love is of God..."

Our Father in heaven, hallowed be Thy name. We Your children are honored to call upon You Whenever we are lonely and sad. Please create in us a clean heart so that we will listen to Your words of comfort and encouragement. Thank You for the prophets who spoke gloriously about You. We are asking You to be our guide and deliverer when the enemy of our soul strikes. Help us to be kind to each other as we reflect Your glory. Amen!

Yvonne Edwards

Lessons I Learned About Loving Myself

I am dark but beautiful, O women of Jerusalem – dark as the tents of Kedar, dark as the curtains of Solomon's tents.
Solomon 1:5

When I was growing up, I despised my dark skin, my high cheekbones, and my prominent lips. I spent a great deal of time, with my lips tucked in, as I shamefully hid them. My high cheekbones and my dark skin made me appear to resemble the natives from the Continent of Africa and I hated myself for being made this way. I disliked my back and vowed never to wear anything that exposed it. I just wasn't comfortable in my skin, never really liked what I saw in the mirror.

Over the years, I learned to love myself, but it did not come easy, it's been a real journey, and every step of the way God showed me that I am beautiful.

These are the lessons I learned about myself:

- *My dark skin, my smooth silhouette glistens like the moon in the twilight, I am one color, black all over and I love it.*
- *My high cheekbones, all five of my babies loved to rest on them, with just a touch of my baby's brow I can detect a fever better than any thermometer.*
- *I learned to appreciate these cheeks that guided my babies through many illnesses. I love my sensitive cheekbones*
- *My prominent lips are a seductive sweetness my husband can't resist. I learned to love the apple shape of my lips.*
- *My back is a story all by itself.*

When I was having my daughter, I had to have an emergency C-Section. Which meant I had to show my back for the epidural to be inserted but I didn't care, having a healthy baby meant more than my shame. As the anesthesiologist looked at my back while giving me the epidural, he said "Your back is perfect." I never forgot that day when he said that.

Even today I still won't show my back, but over the years I have learned to respect the strength of it, for it has borne many burdens, many tears, many stripes. I have been beaten down many times but because God is on my side, and because of the strength of my perfect back, I am still standing. My features are African, and I have grown to love that I am an African queen.

I still don't spend much time in the mirror, that's just not me. But I do love to look at my developing young daughter, as I remind her daily that she is beautifully made by God.

Heavenly Father, clothe Your daughters of Zion with Your divine glory and fill us with the power of the Holy Spirit. For only then will we understand that we are fearfully and beautifully made by You. Amen!

Pastor Latoya Smythe-Forbes

God's Word

"Heaven and earth shall pass away but my words shall not pass away." Matt. 24:35

As the galaxies remain in the heavens and as earth rotates on its own axis, God's word is sure, unchanging, and never fails. It is to be trusted without doubt. It is to be believed without fear. It is to beloved without hate; and it is to be cherished with gladness. It is to be understood with contrition and forgiveness, knowing that the word is God full of mercy and grace with a desire to illuminate the mind to accept his gift of salvation.

God's word is the foundation of society, from the smallest unit of the family to the largest unit of government. Unfortunately, in today's world, God's word appears to have been put on the back burner while society struggles in a lesson of futility to solve problems, while deliberately ignoring God's word which has the answer to its problems. 2 Chronicles 7:14 states "If my people who are called by my name shall humble themselves, and pray, and seek my face, and turn from their wicked ways; then will I hear from heaven, and will forgive their sin, and will heal their land."

God's word is not fiction, it is always truthful and once uttered does not return void. God's word is the bulwark that never fails. It is the rock of our salvation that we build our faith upon. It is the anchor we must never let go of, as it keeps our ship in place so that we do not sink. God's word is a comfort to the soul who is agonizing with God for deliverance in the dark lonely hours of the night. God's word is the spiritual food that a mother feeds upon, when she has no money to pay the rent, buy food or clothes for her children and in danger of losing her livelihood. God's word is the unseen substance that men of old held onto in their deep trials and tribulations? It bolstered their zeal and desire to serve Him and to know that God is real and has never failed. His word is the balm in Gilead that soothes every soul.

Upon studying the life of the Apostle Paul, we see God's word through His transforming power profoundly impact Paul's life. It is further amplified by the fact that Paul went from being the persecutor to the persecuted, it was ironic. Paul ensconced himself in the word, built himself a spiritual fortress by which, he could not be shaken from his faith. The word was made manifest through diligent study and practice, in addition to a serious adherence to its principles. It yielded positive fruits, a change in lifestyle and character. Paul became one of the most revered spiritual leaders in his lifetime and posthumously since his death, many centuries ago.

God's word was never designed to condemn mankind to death, but rather to be instrumental in developing a loving daily relationship, through communication with God in the study of His word. Thereby, opening the intellect through knowledge and the application of wisdom in order to fight against the rulers of darkness in this world. God's word is the power of our salvation, to strengthen us when we are weak, to call on heaven's angels to assist us when

we are about to fall or have fallen. God's word is our daily bread from which we derive our spiritual strength.

Heavenly Father, God of the Universe, help me to communicate with You daily through the study of Your word. Help me to diligently apply Its principles to my life, help me to live a pure life which is befitting as a citizen for Your future kingdom.

Faith D. Housen

Who Is Your Friend?

When Jesus saw how much faith they had, He said to the crippled man, "My friend, your sins are forgiven." Luke 5: 20, CEV.

"Grandma" was a cat with a long black tail and full white body. She got this name after her third set of kittens. At our new house, this cat use to pass through the backyard as she went about her business. Sometime later she got pregnant and continued with her routine.

One morning, a few weeks later, we woke up to the sounds of kittens under a black drum in the backyard. As the kittens grew, she moved them into our carport filled with junk. Every day like any caring mother, she would leave her babies and go hunting and returned with their food. Eventually, she weaned them and went her way.

Seeing what had happened, we started to feed the two kittens. The male had a black tail with two black strokes on its forehead. We named him "Whitie." His sister had a coat of black and white we called her "Blackie." After we had fed them for months, they became tame and grew up to be nice cats. Then "Blackie" got pregnant.

Time went by and one evening when I went out to feed them, "Blackie" was absent, and I figured that she had had her kittens. Night came and we retired. At about 3 a.m., I got up to get a cup of tea. To my surprise, "Whitie" was on the ladder peeking into the kitchen and meowing persistently. Wondering about his actions, I asked my husband to open the door. "Whitie" quickly rushed to the door and by his actions, he was saying "Blackie" has had her babies and she is hungry. We fed her. We were amazed to see a cat playing the role of a human being.

In the story found in Luke 5:17-21, CEV, Jesus was teaching a multitude. Friends of a crippled man heard about His healing power and brought their friend on his sick bed to be healed. But the crowd prevented them from getting into the house. They went up on the roof where they made a hole and let down the man in front of Jesus. Jesus, seeing their faith, said to the man, "My friend, your sins are forgiven." The man picked up his mat and went his way praising God.

Friends, we do not have to be crippled by sin any longer. Jesus, our dearest Friend, left the splendor of heaven, came to earth, suffered, bled, died, was resurrected, and ascended to heaven where He is pleading for us. He says, "Friend, your sins are forgiven. You are healed and set free. Get up out of your bed of affliction! Go tell the good news and praise the Lord.

Dear God, whoever reads this article, please help them not to be crippled emotionally, mentally, or physically with any form of

affliction. Help them to grow in faith knowing that with You, all things are possible. Amen!!!

Bula Haughton-Thompson

God's Grace Gives Us A New Start

It is grace you have been saved, through faith-and this not from yourselves, it is the gift of God-not by works, so that no one can boast. Paul tells us in Ephesians that it is grace that saves us. God's amazing grace, God's undeserved favor, has the power to save a wretch like me. It's a gift from God. We can't earn it, we can't buy it; we can't qualify for it, we can't save-up for it, we can't deserve it. And we certainly can't boast about the fact that we have it. Eph. 2:8-9

It's probably one of the most chilling sensations in the world. You're driving along in your car on an open freeway, clear nighttime driving conditions, cheerful, absorbing music blaring out to all four speakers, all 8-cylinders zipping you along. You're having a great time.

Suddenly, you look in your mirror. And that red light is there!

That terrifying red light. You can't see the rest of the patrol car; you can't see the police officer-not yet. Just that glowing red light.

And you know you're caught. Wow, you were driving seventy-five, maybe even eighty...in a 55 MPH speed limit. You just weren't thinking about it. You are caught. You are nervous, you are sweating, and wondering what's next. You grumbled, this is going to cost me, maybe two hundred dollars, plus traffic school, maybe an increase in my insurance rates. That red light in my rearview mirror means nothing but never-ending heartbreak.

The officer comes up to my window: he is very courteous, very professional. He looks at my driver's license and my registration. There is a long moment while I waited....

And then suddenly, the officer looks down at me and says, "Donna, I'm not going to give you a ticket this time. But please slow down, OK?"

I'm off the hook, No ticket, No traffic school, No punishment, No insurance problems. I've been forgiven. What I have experienced is GRACE. And that wonderful feeling of relief and freedom is just a tiny slice of grace-God's Amazing grace.

As I reflect on my life experiences, a stowaway under the bottom of a ship, robbed by four gunmen at my home, hit by a huge cement truck on the highway, financial challenges, and the list goes on, I can confidently shout "It is only by God's Grace" that

I am still standing. I give God all the praise and glory for His matchless grace. Through His grace I can experience a new start.

Eternal Father, thank You for always showing up in my situations even when I don't deserve it. Thank You for Your amazing grace that wipe out all my problems and give me a brand-new start in Jesus' name. Your constant love and renewed mercies are amazing. In the Precious name of Jesus. Amen!

Dr. Donna Barrett

But my God shall supply all my needs according to His riches in glory by Christ Jesus. Phil. 4:9. God is our refuge and strength, a very present help in trouble. Psalm. 46 :1.

Today, I am blessed to share this testimony of one of the many ways Jesus has worked in my life in answer to prayer. This experience has helped me and strengthened me in my spiritual walk. It has also helped me to increase my trust in Jesus.

Some years ago, one of my daughters was diagnosed with cancer. During this time, I see the hand of God working mightily in our lives. Very often I borrow the words of Lidie H. Edmunds in one of her songs, *"My faith has found a resting place, not in a man-made creed. I trust the Ever-living One, His wounds for me shall plead."* I called my daughter Jay for this time. Jay had an appointment with the oncologist. This appointment was to discuss treatment, procedure, and costing. There was a procedure that was to be done following the first sets of treatment. Following the discussion, the doctor said he has three available dates to choose from and he proceeded to give me the dates. During this time, I have been talking to my Father for direction and help. Trusting in the promises of God by faith in God as my Provider, I opted to the first date. My daughter looked at me with tears in her eyes as if she is saying where is that money coming from at this time and just to let you know, my daughter was in university at the time, and I am a single mother. But thank God, He reminded me instantly that, *"before you call, I will answer and while you are yet speaking, I will hear." And of course, God is always an on-time God.*

Quietly, I was talking to God. On my way home my phone rang, this was a family friend trying to find us. She said she was coming by to drop something off. She came and handed me an envelope and told me not to open until after she left because it was small. As soon as she left, I opened the envelope, and it was about a quarter of the money needed. I called my daughter and we thanked God for answering while I was yet speaking to Him. My friend, I must let you know that by the following Sunday, I had all the money to pay the doctor, for transportation and for us to have lunch.

I can confidently say that my God is an on-time God, and His promises are true, so trust Him always and He will fulfill His promises in our lives.

Dear Heavenly Father, I ask that You allow this devotional thought to help strengthen someone's faith in You. Remind us Lord that You say in Your words to Call upon Me and I will

shew you great and marvelous things that ye know not of. May each reader be blessed by my experience. Amen!

Celeste Gunter

The Holy Spirit

"And whosoever shall speak a word against the son of man it Shall be forgiven him, but unto him that blasphemeth against the Holy Ghost it shall not be forgiven." Luke 12:10

The Trinity of the Godhead includes three distinct individuals, God the Father, God the Son and God the Holy Spirit. They are not independent of each other; they co-exist as one; and unite for the common goal of saving souls for the kingdom of heaven.

The Holy Spirit's function in the role of the Godhead is to convict men's hearts spiritually to accept Christ as their personal savior. He does not use force or pressure. He gently taps on an open receptive heart's door, wooing the individual with love and kindness towards the Savior's saving grace. The Holy Spirit gives many warnings and sometimes premonitions to the soul that is hardening its heart. The urgent message is for that soul to change its way before it is too late. The Holy Spirit tries to capture the mind through unfaltering truths, and life's experiences of other individuals who, failed to take heed to serious warnings, which ultimately resulted in death to a Christ less grave. Furthermore, the Holy Spirit acts as a catalyst in presenting our prayer requests before God the Son as He intercedes for us at the throne of grace before God the Father. The Holy Spirit translates our requests into intelligible language that is acceptable to God the Father and Son. Their main objective in uniting as one is for the saving of the human soul, to be reunited with Christ forever more at the return of his second coming upon whom the second death will have no effect.

In understanding how the Holy Spirit works in the lives of men, let us briefly review two biblical characters who have gone down in the historical annals of history, Pharaoh and Jezebel in comparison to Peter and Paul. Pharaoh and Jezebel were unwilling to yield their lives to God. They cynically questioned who He was. They displayed a haughty spirit of pride, unforgiveness, spitefulness and hard heartedness. They believed in themselves as accountable to no one because of their riches. They did not believe in the God of Israel or the universe. They practiced idolatry and openly displayed their contempt to God. God knew their hearts and with each rejection of the Holy Spirit they permanently shut heaven's doors from remaining open to them. In contrast Peter and Paul, once converted submitted their will to the Holy Spirit, to follow Christ

and lived lives that were the best witnesses of him. They took the saving of their soul's salvation very seriously and did not want to grieve the Holy Spirit in any manner. They did not want to live their lives in abject shame or disgrace, they did not want to reject the Holy Spirit but wanted to be examples to others of

God's amazing saving grace. We too like them, must decide to accept and follow the path where the Holy Spirit leads, in order to be saved in God's kingdom.

Dear Father, up in Heaven, please keep heaven's doors open to me by yielding my will in accepting the Holy Spirit. Amen!

Faith D. Housen

An Unusual Walk

I am the Light of the world. He that followeth me will never walk in darkness but shall have the light of life. John 8:12 (KJV)

The air was balmy with a tinge of the nearby lapping Cayman Sea in it. All nature was stirring as the last rays of the golden westering sun peered through the surrounding nimbostratus clouds. I looked up and in contrast was clear sky above!

Intentionally, I slowed my pace to add more enjoyment to my evening walk down the windswept street which was lined with parched sea grape leaves from nearby trees. Melodious sounds of chirping birds flitting from tree to tree coupled with squawking Cayman parrots was music to my ear. My merry feathered friends were attempting to settle in the best roosting spots thus ending their day simultaneously with the setting sun. I gasped to my husband, "What a Wonderful Creator!"

I quickly realized that nature was teaching some very compelling lessons amidst the doom and gloom of the Corona Virus (COVID-19). The setting sun appeared to be saying that our God will certainly continue to be our constant Guiding

Light, just as it sets each evening and rises anew every morning. Additionally, the clear sky overhead was a stark reminder that there is hope from above, our God is omnipresent and will be with us in every situation despite storms. My feathered friends were joyfully indicating that gratitude at the end of each day for the minutest things brings contentment and happiness.

Finally, just as the golden lining was dispelling darkness when it peered through those heavy clouds, we too can still shine through the darkness of fear, uncertainty, and despair. Our Eternal Light always shines through us and brightens our lives and gives us guidance, happiness, and contentment along the way. We will all have the opportunity to meet our Great Light of the world as the golden morning approaches. Certainly, darkness will disappear as we see the beams of the golden morning shining brighter and brighter.

Prayer: Our Father in Heaven, You see, hear, and know the beginning and ending. Thank You for always being with us even through the dark valleys of shadows. Lord, continue to be our Guiding Light and give us eye salve so we can see clearly, despite apparent darkness. May we always shine as stars forever in your Son's name. Amen

Carol Nyack nee Gopaul

Waiting and Surrendered

But if we hope for what we do not see, we eagerly wait for it with perseverance. Romans 8:25, NKJV

Waiting can be incredibly hard. It also depends on what we are waiting for and how long we have been waiting. If we are waiting for a bus or train and they run frequently, we are not likely to feel much anxiety, even if we just missed one. However, if we miss a bus or train, the next one isn't due for another three hours, and we must be at work within an hour, we are likely to be worried and start frantically searching for other options, like Uber or Lyft.

Prayer, faith, and submission are essential disciplines and characteristics of the Christian faith. When we start praying about an issue, we may be filled with excitement about the journey we are about to embark on, particularly the destination: the answer to our prayer. We enthusiastically claim Bible promises, sing lustily, and believe that faith is the victory that overcomes the world, and fast several times. We may even tell others who are praying along with us or know of our prayer requests that we want God's will to be done in the matter. These are all good things that we should do. But what happens when we have been praying for weeks and months, not to mention years, without seeing the fulfillment of our prayers? Many Christians give up praying out of frustration or take matters into their own hands to try to solve the problem. Does that sound like you? Regrettably, that has also been my experience.

When situations like this occur, we or others may assume that we didn't have enough faith, or we may feel like we have expended all our physical, mental, spiritual, and emotional strength and have nothing left to continue praying and believing. What do we do then? Submit! Submit the matter to God believing that He has heard all our prayers and seen our efforts. Now, instead of claiming the promises for what you want, claim the promises that God knows and wants what is best for you. Trust that His plans for your life will be infinitely better than your own. Trust that He will make all things beautiful in His time and that His timing will be perfect for you. Remember Abraham? He did it his way, not waiting on God to provide a son for him with Sarah. He reaped the bitter consequences. Thankfully, he learned from this mistake. When faced with the bigger test of sacrificing Isaac, he submitted to God, not knowing the outcome. He became known as the father of the faithful. Faith and submission (surrender) go hand in hand.

Dear God, strengthen my faith in You to bless me and provide for me as You see fit. Help me not to become discouraged and abandon my faith in You when my prayers aren't answered immediately or as I expected. Rather, help me to follow Jesus' example of praying not my will, but Your will be done. I submit my needs and the desires of my heart to You, in Jesus' name and for His sake. Amen!

Susan Gay

Serving God Through Serving Others

And the King shall answer and say unto them, verily I say unto you, inasmuch as ye have done it unto the least of these my brethren, ye have done it unto me. Matt. 25:40 (KJV)

There are times when we have our own idea of how we should spend our days, not regarding that our life is in God's hands. We pray and ask the Lord to direct our steps and make us a blessing to someone, but then try to dictate to God exactly how that should take place. But our loving Savior is patient with us and gently reveals to us His plans in a way that we cannot be mistaken.

It was Women's Day. I was not a happy camper. I tried to get the entire Sabbath off, but I couldn't. I would have to work the evening shift. I was thankful to be off in the morning so I can worship with the other women and listen to the Presentation from the Women's Ministries Director of our Conference. I was a new Women's Ministries Director myself and was really enjoying the ministry. I shared with her my disappointment of not being able to be at the afternoon session. She said to me, maybe God wants you to do something for someone today that only you can do.

My afternoon at the nursing facility began the usual way. At around 9pm I went into Mr. R's room to administer his routine medication and he suddenly started pouring his heart out to me. This nursing facility was his permanent residence now. His wife and son came to visit very often, but this weekend his wife was out of town to attend one of their granddaughter's graduation exercise, and his son was out of the State on a business trip, so he was all alone and felt very depressed. I remained with him for about half an hour and actively listened as he spoke about his life with his wife and how he missed her so much, now that he had to remain in the nursing facility. He said he loved her unconditionally and felt very unhappy not being able to hold her in his arms to go to sleep. He expressed that his heart hurt when she would leave at the end of her visits and all he could do was cry; and cried he did as he held my hand.

By this time my own heart was hurting, and a lot of thoughts were going through my mind as I sat in the chair next to his bed. What if this was me in that bed? How would I have dealt with this situation? Mr. R then thanked me for staying and listening to him. He asked God to bless me and said to me that he talks to God night and day. As he stroked my hand he said, I am glad that you were here tonight, and then asked if I was coming back the next day. I said, "yes, by the grace of God." As I left the room, I heard the words of the Women's Director's voice in my ear. I breathed a prayer. Thank you, Lord, for this wonderful opportunity to be your servant tonight.

Heavenly Father, thank You for your promise to instruct us in the way in which we should go. Thank You for Your Holy Spirit prompting us to obey. Amen.

Sharon Roberts

Yes, No, Maybe So

Your ears shall hear a word behind you, saying, "This is the way, walk in it," Whenever you turn to the right hand or whenever you turn to the left. Isaiah 30:21 (NKJV)

We are always required to make decisions. They can include what to wear or what meal to prepare. That was my dilemma recently. I usually decide beforehand what to prepare for breakfast, but that morning was different. I stood there with the refrigerator's door wide opened, and my mind blank. I could not decide what to prepare for breakfast. What made it so interesting is that I had done my full grocery shopping the day before, so the refrigerator, pantry, and cupboards were well stocked. I am sure some of you share a similar experience. One of my many nieces did almost the same thing when she was younger. She would often open the refrigerator or cupboard and exclaim, 'Mom, I don't know what to eat.' Sometimes it is not easy to decide, whether it is from several options or between two options.

Joshua invited the children of Israel, on the verge of entering the promised land, to choose between two options, "Choose for yourselves this day whom you will serve, whether the gods which, your fathers served that were on the other side of [a]the River, or the gods of the Amorites, in whose land you dwell. But as for me and my house, we will serve the Lord." Joshua 24:15 (NKJV). When faced with the decision, Joshua decided that he and his family would serve the Lord.

Similarly, when faced with the choice of returning to her idolatrous homeland or accompanying her mother-in-law Naomi to Judah, Ruth chose the latter. As a result, Jesus was born through her lineage. (Ruth 1: 5-6). Little did she know the far-reaching effects of her decision. Isaiah 30:21 is a reminder that God will both speak to us and direct in all our ways and choices if we only listen and allow Him to lead.

Dear Lord, I surrender my all to You today. Please help me to listen and follow as You speak to me and lead my life in Jesus' name. Amen!

Annette L. Vaughan

God Cares

Jesus Wept. John 11:35, NKJV

It can be difficult to discern God's love amidst grief and sorrow; yet God promises never to leave nor forsake us (*Deuteronomy 31:8*). He promises that when we go through life's afflictions, He will be with us (*Isaiah 43:2*). The death of a loved one is often a difficult experience to live through. When my Dad died on August 31, 2019, it was painful and one of the most sorrowful experiences of my life. However, I also witnessed the most powerful demonstrations of God's providence and love in the circumstances related to his death.

My cousin Gabriel and his family went to Dad's home to finalize travel plans for a trip he was planning to the U.S. to visit me. Gabriel realized that something was wrong with Dad and eventually took him to a clinic where he suffered a stroke, went into a comma, and was rushed to the hospital. My Dad lived alone and most likely would have died alone during the night if Gabriel and his family had not gone to his home that night. Because of the close relationship I shared with my Dad, it would have caused me more sorrow to know that my Dad was found dead in his home. I saw God's mercy, providence, and love for my Dad and our family in how He arranged those events in sending Gabriel to assist Dad.

The day that I got the news that my Dad was hospitalized, and subsequently died, I was in another state spending the weekend with the Jepsons, a wonderful Christian family. Again, I saw God's providence related to that visit. I had made plans on three previous occasions to visit them, but each time, I had to cancel the trip, mostly due to wintery weather. I later realized that God had arranged for me to be with that family, as opposed to being alone, the weekend my Dad died. The fellowship, prayers, and loving support they provided were exactly what I needed at that time. But God wasn't done with demonstrating His amazing love during this difficult time. He impressed my friend Joel to drive up from Texas to help me get home to Barbados as quickly as I could. Joel helped me find an airline ticket, paid for it, advised me about how to quickly wrap up things at work, helped with domestic tasks, and drove me to Austin, Texas in the middle of the night to catch a flight to Florida, from where I would leave for Barbados the next day. God knew that I was so overcome with grief and overwhelmed with all that had to be done, that He sent a friend, who didn't ask if he could help, but who just showed up to help.

Talk about God's amazing providence and love! Though I continue to mourn the death of my Dad, I do so with the certainty of God's love based on the evidence He provided during a time of unbearable grief.

Dear God, comfort me as I go through trials, pain, and grief. Provide evidence of Your loving care and remind me that You cry when I cry, and You hurt when I hurt. Give me faith and strength to believe Your promises, in Jesus' name and for His sake, I pray. Amen!

Susan Gay

His Purpose for My Life

Whether therefore ye eat, or drink, or whatsoever ye do, do all to the glory of God. 1 Cor. 10:31 KJV

One Saturday morning, I got out of the house early to do a special litany performance at church. I was leaving early but was still in a rush in order to beat everyone there.

The roads were still wet from an earlier rain fall. I wanted to turn left at the light before it turned, so I accelerated as the light changed to yellow. On the turn, the car skidded, and I lost control. I hit a curb hard. I pressed on the brakes, but they were gone. With the car still accelerating, it hopped over the median to the other side of the road, with no immediate on-coming traffic (Praise God!), rode up another curb and hit a tree.

A tow truck seemed to arrive in seconds and the ambulance very soon after that. The paramedics would not believe me when I said I was fine until they ran all the necessary test, and all my vital signs were as they should be. I had been pulled out of my car without a scratch on me. My car, on the other hand, was totaled. The tree was dented, but still standing firm.

I cannot begin to fathom why some people can survive such as ordeal and why others do not. What I can tell you is that I was not going to waste my wake-up call. Earlier that year, I had been going through a lot emotionally and was beginning to question what my purpose was. That day I got my answer, as long as I have breath, I am to serve God to the best of my ability.

Once I was cleared to leave, I called my friend, Nicole to come and get me. I got to church on time and performed the litany with all my heart, mind, and strength.

Lord, help me to remember that my purpose is to live for You. Amen!

Christine Thompson

Forgiveness

If you forgive those who sin against you, Your heavenly Father will forgive you. But if you refuse to forgive others, your Father will not forgive your sins. Matthew 6:14 & 15 (NLT).

I used to think that when I forgive someone who offends me, they gained the power and would laugh at me. After going through periods of infidelity during my marriage, years later I was shocked with the news of my best friend bearing a child for my then husband. When this news hit me 19 years later, I was overwhelmed with a flood of emotions. In my mind, this was an unforgivable act! No way could I imagine forgiving a best friend whom I trusted for so many years of my life.

During the grieving process, I turned to God and begged him not to allow me back in that dark slippery valley that I had become so familiar with. I knew very well what that journey was like. My soul was exhausted!! I could not think of anything else that could have been worse. I reached out to a few close friends who cried with me, prayed with me, and listened as I mourned the loss of my friend. I struggled with the thoughts of what the journey ahead would look like and how my children and I would navigate our way through what seemed like an impossible future.

With the passage of time, I found healing through God. My smile and laughter returned, I wanted to live, I experienced freedom and joy so much that I was excited to reach out to my offender and offer grace and forgiveness. I made the phone call but no answer. I was disappointed. Then I wrote an email and still to date no response. I was relieved however, that my spirit was free and hoped that my former best friend felt forgiven.

Is there someone who have wronged or offended you? Maybe it was intentional, or maybe they're not aware that they've caused you hurt. No matter what the circumstance, as believers, we are called to forgive. This is NOT easy but what I know for sure, our Heavenly Father is willing and able to equip you with the tools necessary to do so if you ask Him.

Choosing forgiveness doesn't excuse the other person's behavior. It simply releases you of the burdens of anger and bitterness. Forgiveness opens the door so that you can walk free. Choose freedom today by choosing forgiveness.

"Father, today I seek Your love by choosing forgiveness. I open my heart and ask You to heal my hurts. I look forward to the future You have for me. Help me to be a testimony of Your love and forgiveness to others in Jesus' name. Amen!

Georgia Douglas

Trusting In God

"Commit thy way unto the Lord; trust also in him, and he shall bring it to pass." Psalm 37:5

Trusting in God is to lay your body prostrate at his feet, baring your soul and exposing your vulnerabilities. To trust in God is to lay down your burdens, give him your fears, worries, and problems. It is to acknowledge I am weak, and you are strong. Please, Dear Lord rescue me for I cannot do it alone.

Trust in God develops over time as a result of experience from the School of Hard Knocks. The trust is fulfilled after deep agonizing over difficult situations, the removal or may be not of physical and mental roadblocks, constant door closures when pleading with God for a break, loneliness, and the vicissitudes of life's processes to name a few. Trust according to God's will is made complete when the petitioner through persistent prayer is able to say like Job, "though he slays me yet will I trust him." No matter what life's experiences and consequences have been, it is the recognition that God is God of all, He is the answer to every situation and his will is to be accepted without question or doubt.

I met a gentleman as a student at Oakwood College. He had labored very hard to give all his children a Seventh day Adventist Christian Education from grade school through college. I was very impressed with his testimony he described. The difficulties he had experienced to make his dream a reality. He concluded his testimony by stating upon achieving their Education, his children walked away from the Lord and their faith. Sadness and disappointment for a fleeting second etched across his face but discouraged no he was not. He smiled as he admonished me as a young student to trust in God always, especially when the difficult times arise. He stated if he had to raise his children all over again, he would do it all again with no exceptions, even if he knew beforehand that his children would turn away from God. His outlook on life, was God is a good God who had never failed him yet. He had developed a relationship with God that had been cemented and bonded by faith and trust. Like Job this gentleman was truly able to say, "though he slays me yet will I trust him."

Dear Heavenly Father, help us to develop a trusting relationship with You through the daily medium of communication of prayer. Stimulate our minds, help us to develop the art of listening to that still small voice of the Holy spirit; and as we submit our will to His will, we will be able to lead by example like Job.

Faith D. Housen

Unashamed Hope

Hope deferred maketh the heart sick: but when the desire cometh, it is a tree of life. Proverbs 13:12 KJV

As a young girl, I always prayed to get married and own a home. Truth be told, the desire to have children has only fluctuated periodically in my head, but I was sure of the husband that I would marry then buy a home and build our life together. One night, God told me who I would marry.

Eventually, I grew up, decided to move out on my own and chose to rent for a year or two until the man arrived.

Well, it's been ten years later. Still renting and still no husband. The frustration and struggle are real. Love and loss are painful. Over the years, I let it all get to me, which have caused heartbreak, bitterness, and sorrow. I have made so many mistakes during this wait. Doubting God and want to take matters into my own hands while others are walking down the aisle and starting their lives. One year it was six couples, two of which were my related to me.

I can only imagine Abraham and Sarah's similar frustration and discomfort. Hoping and trusting in a promise that took decades to be fulfilled. Making mistakes all in the name of having their promise realized.

Through time and experience I have learned that God's timing is perfect. When I trust in God, I find I can wait more patiently, and loneliness diminishes greatly. When I trust, believe, and hope I am being true to God and by doing that, I am being true to myself. This may not be the typical happy ending that we have grown to expect, but I'm happy because it is not the end. My promise is still on it's way.

Lord, thank You for never making a promise that You can't keep. Amen!

Christine Thompson

Serving God through Serving Others

Peter replied, "Repent and be baptized, every one of you, in the name of Jesus Christ for the forgiveness of your sins. And you will receive the gift of the Holy Spirit." Acts 2:38 (KJV)

I recently taught Composition writing to a group of 11-year-old students. As I was doing my research, in preparation for the lessons, I found a handy acronym to help them remember how to revise their compositions: ARMS. A stands for Add sentences and words, R stands for Remove Un-needed words and sentences, M stands for move a sentence or placement and S stands for substitute words and sentences for others.

As I reflected on the lesson, I realized that God wants us to use ARMS, too, but not to revise our lives but to allow Him to create a new life in us as we work for others. While I was focusing on helping students learn how to successfully pass an important examination, I had missed the opportunity to share how they could write their own life story with Jesus at the helm. Peter, one of the disciples, didn't miss such an opportunity. He was bearing arms for Jesus in Jerusalem on the day of Pentecost. He, along with the other disciples, who were filled with the Holy Spirit, testified of Jesus to the people there of every "nation under heaven" (Acts 2:5).

If we read Acts 2:37, we note that when the people heard them, "they were pricked in their heart, and said unto Peter and to the rest of the apostles, Men and brethren, what shall we do?" Peter replied, "Repent and be baptized, every one of you, in the name of Jesus Christ for the forgiveness of your sins. And you will receive the gift of the Holy Spirit."

God wants to Add the Holy Spirit to our lives in full measure. When the Spirit comes on our Day of Pentecost, He Removes all sin, Moves unnecessary people and things from our lives and Substitutes His life for ours. Now, we can write our very best story – a life hid in Christ.

I have not always served God to His name's honor and glory. But I am thankful for the opportunity to repent, be baptized, and receive forgiveness for my sins. Thank God for the gift of the Holy Spirit. You too have an opportunity to revise your story as you remember the acronym: ARMS.

Heavenly Father, thank You for giving me the opportunity to revise the script of my life. Send Your Holy Spirit to empower me so that my life can be a story that testifies of Your love and grace. In Jesus' name, Amen!

Debbie Bovell

Listen to The Spirit

A wise man will hear, and will increase learning; and a man of understanding shall attain unto wise counsels: Proverbs 1:5

Have you ever had a best friend to whom you could confide everything? I have such an earthly friend. Her name is Debbie. We were study partners together during our graduate program and have remained steadfast friends ever since. Our joys and sorrows are shared and wherever we have challenges, we know that we can call each other and find human help in time of need. But, as wonderful as human friends are, they have limitations. Not every promise will be kept. Not every bit of advice will be perfect. Even when we mean well circumstances may intervene and the best plans to assist can be foiled. Not so with the Holy Spirit. He is the best of best friends.

He is ever-present and we can have His help in a constant and wise supply. He never gets weary, and the communication costs us no more than thought and time. He is attuned to our every need before we know it and can guide us out of danger if we will only ask and follow the advice given.

A special case in point was a day I took my son to the doctor. He was very young at the time and I took him to seek the pediatrician because he was ill. I was not feeling well myself and the doctor noticed. She said she would give me something to take after examining me and it would save me from having to visit the doctor next door. I was very happy as we had waited long to see her, and I wanted to get home to rest. She prescribed an antibiotic and a mucus thinner. I am allergic to several medications and was careful to question whether they could be used together. She affirmed that they could be. I went to the pharmacy after our consultation ended and while the lady was filling the prescription, I asked again if they could be taken together. She said that they could. I asked her to be certain that the leaflet was in each box. She did that, and I took them home. Yet, the Spirit made me uneasy.

As soon as I got into the house, I checked the leaflets. You guessed it! The two medications specified by their names were identified as medicines which, should never be used together. I avoided a serious challenge by listening to the Spirit.

Today, let us listen to the Spirit. His advice is that of the very best Friend. If we listen to Him, we can avoid many difficulties which lie across our paths.

Dear God, it is my desire to listen to Your Spirit. Teach me to know Your voice and heed Your word promptly, so that I may walk in the light you shed on my way for time and eternity. Amen

Jean Trotman

Conquering Our Fears

Have I not commanded you? Be strong and of good courage; do not be afraid, nor be dismayed, for the Lord your God is with you wherever you go. Joshua 1:9 (NKJV)

My husband and I love travelling. Among our travels was a fabulous trip to Geneva, Switzerland with siblings, relatives, and friends. Each day involved a new and exciting adventure which included a tour of some historical place of interest. However, our trip to Chamonix-Mont-Blanc was a day that remains forever etched in my memory. It was the day I bravely faced and conquered my fear of heights.

The route from our hotel in Geneva to the Chamonix-Mont-Blanc was long but very scenic. We passed the time chatting taking photos and joking with each other. Amidst all that, I was quietly panicking. You see, the informational brochure indicated that Mont-Blanc is situated at an elevation of 15, 771 feet (4,807 meters). To reach the summit, we would have to ascend in the highest cable car system in the world. Not only that, once there, we would then walk across a sky bridge that connects the cable car station to Central Piton terrace which is another free-standing rock elevation.

As we approached, Chamonix, my fears intensified, and I began thinking of every possible excuse for opting out. Meanwhile, those in our group as well others waiting in line to ascend all seemed excited. Thus, I choose not to voice my fears or apprehension, but rather, to feed on their enthusiasm and excitement. It worked! When the cable car arrived, I calmly boarded, whispered an earnest prayer, stood in the middle of the group, and deliberately chose not to look down. Well, even if I had done so, it would not have made much of a difference because something amazing occurred, God sent a mist in the valley that shrouded the depth and allowed for a less fearful and more comforting ride. Furthermore, I also crossed that dreaded bridge without even realizing it due to the density of the mist.

This experience reminds me of the story of the twelve spies when Joshua sent them to assess Canaan (Joshua 13:18-20). Ten of them reported fear and obstacles. They strewed negative talk. It is easy to be intimidated or crippled by our fears. However, Joshua and Caleb were driven by courage and faith. They refused to allow the obstacle of fear to dominate their lives. That is what I chose to do. I surrendered my fears to God, allowing my faith and trust in Him to be complete.

Dear Lord, please help me to be strong, to be of good courage and not to be afraid. Thanks for the assurance that You will be with me wherever I go. I claim that promise in my life in Jesus' name. Amen!

Annette L. Vaughan

His Purpose for My Life - I Have Been Called

Before I formed thee in the belly, I knew thee; and before thou camest forth out of the womb I sanctified thee, and I ordained thee a prophet unto the nations. Jer. 1:5

Many people don't have a clue as to why they are here on planet earth. Are you certain that you were meant to be here and that you are not just an accident? I am. You may ask how I can be sure of it. Let me share with you, my certainty.

When my mother was sixteen and yet unmarried, she told God that she wanted to be married and have four children. God answered and gave her the four she wanted. Then came the bonus. You see, I am number five. While she didn't plan me, God planned me. During her pregnancy, she tripped while alighting from a bus. She could have aborted but didn't. During my childhood years, I was sickly. I had stomach problems and at one stage had a bout of pneumonia, during which I slept for many days. Yet God preserved my life. I knew I was His, and so at nine years old I gave Him my life.

I didn't understand all, but I purposed to live for Jesus and represent Him as best as I could. I continued to watch God's preservation of my life. In 2011, I was going to the bedroom to show my sister a lighthouse from the window. I opened the window and before we could get our heads through it, the window fell and severed the top phalanx of the middle finger on my right hand. I realized that it could have been my neck. The hand is disfigured, but the life is saved yet again.

I have purposed that a life so planned, preserved, and protected by the hand of God must serve Him continually. I want to give myself in absolute surrender to God to have Him work in me to will and to do of His good pleasure. Like Cyrus, called before his birth, I am fascinated that Jesus called me specially to come to this earth to be fashioned after the similitude of a palace and to be given a place in heaven. He MUST have me for now and eternity.

Dear reader, God has a purpose for your life too. That purpose is to be utterly His child. Look at the providences in your life. They are not by chance. Give yourself completely to God and watch as He unveils the grand purpose for the present and the ultimate purpose of salvation in the earth made new.

Dear God, I believe I have a purpose determined by You. Show me it and empower me to submit to it entirely to You I pray. Amen

Jean Trotman

His Purpose for My Life - Beyond Borders

"For My thoughts are not your thoughts, neither are your ways My ways, saith the Lord. For as the heavens are higher than the earth, so are My ways higher than your ways, and My thoughts than your thoughts." Isaiah 55:8-9

During my earlier years, I have always found satisfaction in being superbly organized and strategic. Those were qualities that I found to be Christ-like, as well as attributes that I was convinced would lead to tremendous success. After experiencing repeated twists, turns and round-abouts on this journey called 'life,' I can certainly conclude that regardless of how wonderful my ideas may seem, God's plan is bigger and better than mine could ever be.

At the age of seventeen, I became an elementary school teacher. My plan was to educate students in the Caribbean, namely Trinidad and Tobago and to be a source of motivation and inspiration for them. It is evident that He had a greater plan for my life-one that included educating students who live in the US Virgin Islands, US Mainland, China, and various parts of the world.

Had my plans come to fruition, I would not have been blessed to have met and taught so many young, impressionable individuals. As I reflect, both their lives, as well as my own, I have been blessed as a result of these experiences.

Father, you know the plans You have for my life. Help me to be willing to be used by You whenever, wherever, and however you deem best, in Jesus' name - Beverley Monroe

I am a child of the King

Hear the right, O Lord, attend unto my cry, give ear unto my prayer, that goes not out of feigned lips. Let my sentence come forth from thy presence; let thine eyes behold the things that are equal. Psalm 17:1-2

In Psalm 17 King David pleads with the Lord to hear his voice and to preserve him from walking in the path of men in the world; with the hope to preserve him to behold the Lord's face in righteousness. David called on the Lord to listen to his prayer, that his request came out of his feigned lips, but searched the right in him and attend unto his cry.

There is wonder working power in prayers. Prayers grant us the privilege to know who God is, the joy of appreciation and tell of His goodness. God's compassion is new every morning; it is His mercies that we are not consumed because His compassions do not fail. It is good when we call on Him, we need to open our hearts and wait patiently because He is good to those who seek Him daily and wait on Him. God wants us to talk to Him and tell Him what we desire, because He is always ready to share His blessings with us.

We have been there before; oh yes, sometimes in our lives we feel depressed because of what is happening around us. We sometimes want to make changes ourselves, forgetting to seek God in prayer and listen to His counsel. This counsel by Solomon from Proverbs 8: 17 is a good reminder how wonderful and good our Father is. "I love them that love me; and those that seek me early shall find me." God values us so much that He is always here waiting for us to call and depend on Him." This counsel is a reminder that prayer is a direct communication with our Lord and Savior.

Dear Jesus, thank You for Your gospel. You have giving us Your Son, Jesus Christ in sacrifice to show how much You love us and much You want to bless us. Please help us to be good to others just as You have been good to us. In Jesus name I pray. Amen!

Dr. Maryse Desir

Trusting in God #1

"If we know that He hears us, whatever we ask, we know that we have the petitions that we have asked of Him." 1 John 5:15, NKJV

During the days of Ezekiel, God poured out His heart and shared what He wanted to do for His beloved people. Then He revealed an astonishing fact, "I will yet for this be enquired of by the house of Israel, to do it for them" (Eze. 36:37, KJV). God was waiting to be asked!

How many times have we asked of God when it's our last resort? So many times, we rely on ourselves to find the solutions when all we must do, is ask of God.

I think that if there are any tears shed in heaven, they are going to be shed over all the answers to prayer for which no one ever bothered to ask! What blessing is God waiting to give you, but you haven't asked Him for it? Why does He wait for us to ask? Maybe He wants us to acknowledge our need of Him. Maybe it's one way of getting our attention. Maybe it's the only way we will know when the answer comes that it comes from Him, and we don't credit ourselves or someone else for it.

Thank You, Father, for Your promises. Help us to release our faith in You and boldly bring to You all our cares, our joys and our sorrows. Please forgive us where we fall short, Amen!

Trusting in God #2

"Fear thou not; for I am with thee be not dismayed; for I am thy God: I will strengthen thee; yea, I will help thee; yea, I will uphold thee with the right hand of my righteousness." Isaiah 41:10 KJV

A new wave of fear is skyrocketing as the numbers of the 'New Corona Virus' climbs. This virus which has taken the world by storm has the world wondering when it will end. Amid every storm is a calm.

When we think that life is well and good, we sometimes are faced with the most unexpected situations. Today, all can be well and the next day we have the most disturbing and shocking situation to deal with. The Christian path was not promised to be smooth sailing and it's when we are at our lowest then we can trust God the most. It is when we feel that all hope is gone and we can no longer rely on ourselves, then we see how much we need to let go and let God.

It was approximately five years ago when we got the shocking news that my husband was diagnosed with an aggressive prostate cancer which, needed urgent attention. It was in these times that we turned to God for assurance in His words and in prayer. It was at this time in our lives when our friends stood with us in prayers and support and when we found comfort in Isiah 41:10. It was during those times that we experienced God's peace in our lives most, as we realized that our only hope is in Him.

Father we thank You that even through our most difficult situations, even when it seems as if all is lost, we can hold onto Your unfailing promises that the plans You have for us is to prosper us and You will never leave us or forsake us. Please help us to continue trusting You in good times and bad. Amen!

Trusting in God #3

"But I trusted in thee, O Lord: I said, Thou art my God. My times are in thy hand."

Psalm 31:14-15

Have you ever wanted something to happen immediately or in your time frame and you pray and ask God to let it be done as you wish?

One thing I've learned is that God doesn't always work on our timetable. In fact, He rarely does. But in a single moment, God can change our lives! All throughout the scripture, we see examples of how God was working behind the scenes and instantly turned things around for His people. Scripture tells us He is the same yesterday, today and forever, which means if He did it for them, He can instantly turn things around for us too.

Though we may be going through some difficulty today, we can be encouraged because our times are in God's hands. Trust that

He has our best interest at heart. He wants to pour out His favor on us. He wants to take us further than we dreamed possible and work in our lives in ways beyond what we have ever imagined. And while we are waiting, we shouldn't try to figure everything out, as it will only frustrate us.

Let this truth sink down into our hearts today. Resist discouragement by speaking His Word over our future. Keep standing, keep hoping, and keep believing because He is working behind the scenes. Have faith, because our times are in His hands, and He will lead us in the life of the victory He has for us.

Father, today I humbly come before You giving You all that I am. I trust that my times are in Your hands. I trust that You are working things out in my favor. I set my focus on You knowing that You are working things out for my good in Jesus' name. Amen.

Louise Watson-Tomlin

Be Still

Be still and know that I am God. Psalm 46:10

We live in a world filled with chaos, misinformation, problems, sorrow, gloom, sadness, hurt, natural disasters and the list goes on and on. At the writing of this email, we are experiencing a global pandemic with the most recent death toll of over 1.45 million and over 3.8 million cases. Florida, (one of the epicenters) has a total of 389,666 cases with 5,518 deaths (July 22, 2020). We don't have the true number, as many people are not aware that they have the virus (Asymptomatic). Doctor Sanjay Gupta, a medical reporter and writer, stated that many people may have the virus, sometimes for one week before they even experience symptoms.

Before this pandemic, we lived in a world of constant busyness, sometimes we say something like, "there is not enough hours in the day or where did the time go?" or, I didn't get to do all I had planned to do. There are so many things to keep us constantly moving. So many things that are important that we find it difficult to prioritize. We are constantly on the go. In the last three months I have come to realize that so many things are NOT so important.

Let me draw your attention to Psalm 46:10 *"Be still and know that I am God."* As you experience unprecedented times, reminder that God wants us to be still and wait on Him. God does His best work when we are still. You may say, "how can you be still when tragedies are constantly happening? this is exactly what the Lord is saying, "Be still," I got your back, be still, I will never leave you nor forsake you. Be still, I know what you are going through. In fact, He stated, *"Cast all your cares on me because I care for you," Psalm 23:4. "Even though I walk through the valley of the shadow of death, I will fear no evil because Thou art with me, Thy rod and Thy staff They comfort me," Isaiah 43:2."* When you pass through the water, I will be with you and through the rivers, they shall not overflow you, when you walk through the fire, you shall not be burned, nor shall the flame scorch you. Be Still and know that I am God." Again, God is reminding us that He works better when we are still. In the waiting period God wants to refuel, refresh and reestablish us for His will.

Dear Jesus, thank You for reminding us to Be Still so You can work on our behalf. When we surrender to You, the impossible will be accomplished. I cast all my problems on You because You are bigger than anything I experience. Thank you, Lord, for always been there in the most difficult times of my life. My heart is filled with gratitude for Your providence in Jesus' name, Amen!

Dr. Donna Barrett

Thanksgiving

"In everything give thanks: for this is the will of God in Christ Jesus concerning you". 1 Thessalonians 5:18

I have so much to give God thanks for. Without Him I would not be here today. About a year and a half ago, a terrible snowstorm occurred during the day while I was still at work. I was able to leave work early that day. However, there was so much traffic on the road that it caused standstill traffic for many hours. My husband was calling me every half an hour to see how near to home I was. I was finally out of traffic at about 2 AM and was feeling very sleepy. While driving, I fell asleep, and my car started drifting to the other side of the road. My cell phone rang just as I went on the other side. It was my husband calling. I realized what was happening to me as I answered the call and went back in my lane. My husband said he kept hearing a voice saying, "Call Georgia now!" As I told him what happened, we were so thankful he called when he did, or I would have had an accident that night. That voice was God speaking to him.

When I got home that night all we could do was give God thanks for keeping me safe. He saved me from an accident on the road. I am thankful for this life God has given me. In everything give God thanks, not just when things go wrong. He deserves all the praise, honor, and glory.

Dear Lord and Savior of the world, I thank You so much for giving me life, health and strength. Lord, thank You for protection from accidents. I place my entire life in Your hands. Take charge dear Lord and let me always do Your will. In Jesus' name I pray, Amen!

Georgia Alvaranga

Pray Without Ceasing

"Peter therefore was kept in prison: but prayer was made without ceasing of the church unto God for him." Acts 12:5.

Pray without ceasing, "Stay in knee city" was one of the suggestions from our late Sis. Alexander. Amid the storm...be still...in the midst of the challenges...stay connected...in the midst of your problems, pray without ceasing. The Lord will take care of your battles. His ear is not heavy, He will hear you, His hand is not short, He can reach you, His voice is calm and reassuring, you will recognize His sweet voice. He wants to be in a relationship with you, why not allow Him...why not "Be Still" He is ready, He is able! No matter what you are going through, He will never leave you nor forsake you.

This seems to show the power of prayer and how it can help not just us in our troubles, but in every area of our lives. It seems to show that uniting in prayer with others has great power.

When my son-in-law Dex had to do a heart valve replacement surgery, I invited family members, church family, and friends to intercede on his behalf. We established a conference line so that everyone could call in at a scheduled time. We sang, read the scriptures and prayed. At the end of the call, we felt confident that God is in control and that the surgery would go well. The surgery was successful. In fact, one of the surgeons, was very instrumental in the creation of the robotic arm that was used in the surgery. Let us continue to pray without ceasing. He will do what He say we will do. 1 Thessalonians 5:16 "Rejoice always, pray without ceasing, give thanks in all circumstances; for this is the will of God in Christ Jesus for you."

It is not impossible to pray without ceasing. We can do it by intentionally keeping our channels of communication open throughout the day and talk to God. Talk to Him as a friend. Tell Him your likes and dislikes. Ask Him to intervene in your life and help you with the impossible tasks. Give thanks for both small and big things, count your blessings, and celebrate His renewed blessings every morning.

Dear God, in those times when I am tempted to give up, I hear Your still small voice saying that I should continue to pray. Thank You for showing up in my situations. Grant me unwavering faith to pray always whether in good or bad times. Help me to become aware of Your nearness and Your willingness to help me. Saturate my heart with your loving-kindness. Let my life become a never-ending, pray-without-ceasing to You. In Jesus' name. Amen

Dr. Donna Barrett

Trusting in God

But the Lord said to Samuel, "Do not consider his appearance or his height, for I have rejected him. The Lord does not look at the things people look at. People look at the outward appearance, but the Lord looks at the heart." 1 Samuel 16: 7

It's wonderful to know that the Lord we serve do not look at us or measure or treat us by our outward appearance. Jesse had seven sons pass before Samuel, but God did not choose them. Jesse did not even mention to Samuel that he had another son, that Samuel had to ask Jesse if he had only seven sons. Though David's earthly father didn't think much of him, his heavenly father, The Almighty God did think highly of him and that's all that mattered. The Bible says that once the prophet Samuel anointed David, the Spirit of the Lord came mightily on him. David was 17 years old when he was anointed. He became the king of Israel at 30 years old and King David was the most successful king of Israel. Even though David made mistakes along the way, his heart was always in the right place. He loved God with all his heart (Psalms 18:1). When God punished him over Beersheba, He humbly accepted the punishment.

When David was afraid, he put his trust in the Lord. (Psalms 56:3). When the Amalekites made a raid at Ziglag and burnt it and taken captive the women and everyone else, David and his men wept aloud, and his men were bitter. The Bible says that David then encouraged himself in the Lord. Do you know how he encouraged himself? He thought back to the time God helped him kill the lion and the bear. Also, the time he killed Goliath with a sling because he trusted in the Lord in his heart than the giants, he saw in front of him. Today let's be like David and trust God in every situation that we are in. Let's love God with all our heart, soul, spirit, and strength. Let us be obedient to the Lord because the Lord sees it and will honor us at the right time. Let's trust in the Lord with all our heart and acknowledge him in everything that we do so that He may direct our paths.

Heavenly Father, I thank You for seeing me for who and what I am and not like world sees me. Help me to live up to Your standards and forsake worldly ways that's not according to Your will. In Jesus name I pray, Amen!

Sausana Abraham

God Does Care

Be careful for nothing; but in everything by prayer and supplication with thanksgiving let your requests be made known unto God. Philippians 4: 6 AKJV

In Matthew 6:27, Jesus asked, "Which of you by taking thought can add one cubit unto his stature?" As human beings, many of us worry and get anxious to the point of not being able to function properly sometimes. This originated from the Garden of Eden after Adam and Eve fell into Satan's trap. What did they do? Worrying about their nakedness, they made fig leaves aprons for themselves. When we worry, we seek our own solutions and usually we only get more and more frustrated.

For this devotion, I am sharing a personal experience. It is not that I have achieved, or that I am closer to God than others. It is an experience that I am still amazed about. Since September 2016, I have been living alone, but I am thankful. In October last year, all the residents were given notice to seek other accommodation. The owners had to close for renovation and possible selling out and we all had until the end of February to find lodgment somewhere else. Since I was living alone, I really did not want just anywhere, and I preferred not to have an apartment on the ground floor. Of course, I worried about a lot of things, cost and location. Then I decided to talk to God about it telling Him that I am convinced that the same way He supplied where I was at the moment when there seemed to be no hope, that He will provide a suitable place this time again. I asked Him to help me trust Him more. My son helped me search and took me to view apartments, but we were approaching the end of February and we had nothing yet. I did not want to be the last resident to leave.

On Friday evening, February 28th, 2020, at about 3:30, I was going to the washroom, wondering what to do when I heard a voice clearly saying: "Move this week-end." As I said, I lived alone. I was startled, I turned around somewhat scared. Who is that? Immediately, like pushed into action, I called my son and told him: I am going to move on Sunday, check a storage place for me and inquire about availability and cost, and make a reservation for a two-week storage; check also a moving service. It's Friday evening, it will soon be Sabbath. Everything storage, moving van was sorted out before Sabbath as though a well-organized plan was made before. I was baffled, overwhelmed. Could hardly believe that all this had happened in such a short space of time. All I could say is: THANK YOU SO MUCH, LORD, YOU HAVE DONE IT AGAIN!

God knows our needs, He has promised to supply them, He is faithful and true to His promise, He said in His Word that He is not a man that He should lie. I have seen Him at work before, but this time, this clearly audible voice! Nothing is impossible to Him and He knows the inner desires of our hearts, He supplies what is best for us, undeserving though we be. Let us continue to trust Him in everything.

That Friday evening, I did not know yet where I would stay after I had stored my few belongings. Somehow, I did not even think about it during the Sabbath. But my second son came to London on Sunday and there the thought popped up to go to Birmingham with him for the first two weeks of March. While there, in Birmingham, I received a positive answer for one of the flats I had applied for. God had provided once again exactly what I wished.

I pray that this simple testimony can be a source of encouragement for someone this very day. When there does not seem to be any way, remember, God is in control, let us talk to Him, let us trust Him, He will make a way. He cares for the little sparrow, we are more valuable to Him, He will supply what we need.

LET US PRAY: Loving Lord, I thank You for the tangible way You assured me of your care. Help me today and every day to trust You more, help me to learn to allow You to govern my life; You always have everything under control, You will guide me safely and provide what is best for me. In the name of Jesus, I pray! Amen.

Josiane Jones

Blessing is in the Breaking

Taking the five loaves and the two fish and looking up to heaven, he gave thanks and broke the loaves. (AM) Then he gave them to his disciples to distribute to the people. He also divided the two fish among them all. Mark 6:41

It was getting late.

There was a crowd following Jesus to hear his teaching. The disciples asked Jesus to send the crowd away. But Jesus showed compassion towards the crowd as they were there listening and learning, and because they knew Jesus would perform miracles. When Jesus sent the disciples to get food for the crowd, all they could find was 5 loaves of barley bread and 2 fishes. Jesus took the bread and thanked God for it. Notice, Jesus thanked God for the little he had in His hand and broke the bread, knowing fully well that God Almighty, the Great I Am, was in the business of multiplication. May your faith be like that, strong enough to thank God for the little you have in your hand so that God can multiply it. It says the people were satisfied and there were 12 baskets remaining. That's how God blesses! From need to overflow. Being thankful and having faith is the catalyst. God also could have provided that 5 loaves and 2 fish through someone else, a rich person maybe, a prominent person perhaps, or struck it out of a rock but He worked this miracle through the little a small boy had to offer. So today do not think that the little you do for the kingdom of God is not enough in God's sight. God can multiply your efforts no matter how small it is. Let the prayer below be an everyday prayer.

Father God, thank You for the little I have in these times. I believe You can bless me, and I thank You in advance for it. Amen!

Sausana Abraham

God's Providence

Then the word of the Lord came to Elijah: "Leave here, turn eastward, and hide(D) in the Kerith Ravine, east of the Jordan. 4 You will drink from the brook, and I have directed the ravens(E) to supply you with food there." 1 Kings 17:2

The Prophet Elijah had just come back from proclaiming to King Ahab that there would be no rain for the next three years. King Ahab was a wicked king who considered it very trivial to commit sins (1 Kings 16:31) and married Jezebel and worshipped Baal. Imagine the King of Israel forgetting Jehovah God and serving Baal. Jehovah Lord confirmed the word spoken by Elijah in the name of the Most High God by providing for him in the ravine, feeding him through Ravens. This is the Lord we serve. The Lord confirms every word we speak in Jesus' name and provides for us as we continue to do His work in this world. So, let's stand firm and be bold and continue in the work of our Heavenly Father. Whether drought or famine or plague or Covid, the Lord is well able to sustain us!

Father God, in Jesus' name I ask You to work through me to fulfill Your purpose through my life. Amen!

Sausana Abraham

Experiencing the Day of Pentecost in Romania

"And they were all filled with the Holy Ghost, and began to speak with other tongues, as the Spirit gave them utterance... Now when this was noised abroad, the multitude came together, and were confounded, because that every man heard them speak in his own language." Acts 2:4,6

When people talked about speaking in tongues, my mind would always paint a picture of some man or woman speaking in an undecipherable monologue while the congregation shouted and screamed. I associated speaking in tongues with chaos and confusion, until my experience in Romania.

During the communist rule in Romania, I had the journalistic privilege of accompanying the Aeolians on their historic trip to that country. They were a part of the Goodwill Ambassador Program that shared American culture and music with young people living in the Soviet Bloc. Initially, they were slated to travel to Poland but just a few weeks before departure they were informed that the trip to Poland had been cancelled causing them to be reassigned as musical ambassadors to Romania.

Romania??? I was disappointed, I had dreamed of visiting Poland, the land of Lech Wałęsa, and the Solidarity Movement. Nevertheless, we headed to Romania. Little did I know that God was sending me on a Macedonian mission (Acts 16:9). The organizer of the trip set down a cardinal rule that we were expected to respect, No sharing of faith or even the mention of God. Our role was not to proselytize but rather to give them a taste of American culture. We were informed that we could not visit or worship in a Seventh-day Adventist Church. All religious organizations were prohibited by the communist regime. If we abided by this one rule, we would have a memorable trip.

It was a phenomenal tour! We travelled throughout the country. The Aeolians sang in schools, parks, concert halls, wherever people gathered they spontaneously sang. Our weekend itinerary promised to be very special. We were traveling to Constanta, a popular resort on the Black Sea frequented by the elite of the Romanian government.

We started our trip early on Sabbath morning. The scenery was beautiful, but it could not satisfy my longing to be in God's house. Since we didn't have an organized worship service on the bus, I decided that I would study my Bible. I got so engrossed in my study that before I knew it, we were in Constanta.

As soon as we arrived, the bus driver and the hotel personnel began to unload our bags. I was waiting for mine when a tall, blonde man grabbed my bag and said, "Follow me." I was shocked. "You are a Seventh day Adventist, aren't you?" he asked.

"Yes," I answered reluctantly. I wasn't quite sure where this conversation was leading. I didn't know what to make of it. Was he part of Securitate, Romania's notorious secret police? Was this a set up? Once we arrived at my room, he said in a pleading tone, "please teach me the Word." I was taken aback because I knew that I was in a communist country and if I shared my faith, I would risk prison, torture, and maybe death. I didn't answer immediately. I simply told him to come back after dinner and we would talk.

At dinner all I could think about was the tall, blonde stranger and his request. I had to decide. Would I keep silent and deny my faith? Or would I accept to teach him even at the risk of losing my life? I prayed earnestly and asked God to show me what to do. Only God has divine wisdom to discern the hearts and the intents of men. Before I could finish praying God had given me peace, courage, and newfound strength. I determined that whatever the cost, I would teach him. God was with me and I had no reason to fear.

After dinner was over, I returned to my hotel room and who would I see standing beside my door waiting for me with anticipation, the blonde stranger and two young women. I invited them in and with fellow travelers, Rosa and Lance we began to study. The tall blonde stranger introduced himself as Alexander, he was with his wife, Nadia* and her friend, Cristina.*

I was impressed by the Holy Spirit to do a survey of the Bible from Genesis to Revelation. Alexander served as the translator as the ladies didn't speak English. After opening prayer, I began the study while Alexander translated my words. Several minutes after the start of the study, I noticed that Alexander was no longer translating. I stopped and apologized for talking so fast and offered to start again. "No," he replied, "they don't need a translator. They understand you perfectly!" I was simply amazed. I was speaking in English, but they heard me in Romanian with a perfect accent. I was speechless. God is all powerful! Only He could perform such a miracle. My experience reminded me of the apostles on the Day of Pentecost. They spoke in Galileans (Acts 2:7), but the people heard them in their native language. Now God was giving me a Pentecostal experience.

We studied into the night and finally they reluctantly parted but promised to return bright and early in the morning. Before they left, we gave them a Bible. Words couldn't describe their gratitude. It was if we had given them a gold mine. When they left, my friends and I thanked God that He gave us the opportunity to witness to people who were hungering and thirsting after righteousness. I wondered if I had placed them in harm's way, because they stayed so long in my room. It was an unspoken rule that Romanians were not allowed to socialize for long periods of time with foreigners. Wouldn't our fraternizing arouse suspicion? Wouldn't spies denounce them?

I didn't need to worry. God had perfectly planned everything. I just didn't know it. The following day, God answered my questions. We continued our study without a translator and the women again perfectly understood everything. During a break in our studies, they shared a bit of their life story. Alexander was an engineer. He and Nadia had spent most of their time seeking pleasure, but they found no happiness. Through a mutual friend they were introduce to the SDA Church and began to attend church and study the Word. Alexander and Nadia shared their faith with Cristina, who also embraced the Word.

Then God allowed me to see His favor and protection over me. Cristina then told me that her husband was a high-ranking official in the Romanian government. He was at the resort and aware that I was teaching the Bible. Through his wife Cristina, he sent a message to me that I was free to teach the Word but because of his position, he could not enter the room or meet me. God is simply awesome!

We said our final goodbyes and Alexander walked me to the bus. As we were walking, I asked Alexander, "Out of all the people on the bus, how did he know that I was a Seventh day Adventist?"

He smiled with a twinkle in his eyes, "Simple, only an Adventist would carry a Bible on the Sabbath.

"Yes! of course," I laughed. When we arrived in Constanta, I forgot to put my Bible back in my bag. That is how he identified me as a Christian believer.

Thus, Constanta fulfilled the Biblical promise in my life, *"But ye shall receive power, after that the Holy Ghost is come upon you, and ye shall be witnesses unto me both in Jerusalem, and in all Judaea, and in Samaria, and unto the uttermost part of the earth." Acts 1:8*

Today's Prayer: O God for Your glory and honor, today sanctify my tongue that I might share Your love to a dying world. Speak through me Holy Spirit ennoble and sanctify my tongue for Your service. Amen!

*not their real names

Stephanie Johnson-Dingome

His Purpose for My Life

Many are the plans in a person's heart, but it is the Lord's purpose that prevails. Proverbs 19:1 (NIV)

What do you do when you make plans and as life would have it, something happens and all the plans you had made seem now unattainable or even set back dramatically?

The year 2020 wasn't supposed to be this way. This is the year things would change. From the planning of a wedding and where to go for a honeymoon, to moving to a new job, new opportunities, renovating a house into our home as husband and wife, and our first family vacation as husband and wife. It was all set and then came COVID-19. With everything now on hold, all my plans are ruined, or so I thought one cannot go anywhere without a mask, therefore, you can forget about wedding without considering social distancing.

There goes inviting more than 10 people. I suppose you could say I am wondering if anything would go according to plan anymore. How can you make headway when it's not quite clear what the new normal is? I thought when I said *Lord, I really trusted You and when you allowed anything to happen I would trust You did it for my good,* that I really understood what that meant. But sitting here, I am reminded that although this is not what I had planned and all things aren't going the way I wanted, my circumstances may seem confusing but I can place it all in Your hands because your ways are higher than mine. I want mountains to move that you want me to climb but help me to trust Your work, Your will and Your time, because Your ways are higher than mine.

Many times, in life our plans do not follow our leading, but I believe that when God interrupts our planning it is to bring about HIS perfect will in our lives. You may be experiencing this same scenario as you read these words, but I encourage you to keep trusting God's heart. He is never ever wrong, and His ways are always best.

Dear Lord, thank You that even in the midst of all what seems to be chaos and uncertainty, You are still God who sits high yet looks low; and even when things look so dismal You are all I need, and You will see me through. Help me to also remember that Your timing and ways are so much higher and better than mine.

Kay Anne Clarke

My Hope is in the Lord

"For everything that was written in the past was written to teach us, so that through the endurance taught in the Scriptures and the encouragement they provide we might have hope." Romans 15:4

If you are going through trials now, take hope in the fact that almost everyone in the Bible who did great things for God had to endure great hardships. In 2 Corinthians 11: 24-27, Paul recounts many of the difficult circumstances that he had gone though. He received forty lashes. He was beaten with rods, he was stoned, he was shipwrecked. He spent a night and a day in the open sea. Paul was constantly on the move. He was in danger from rivers, in danger from bandits, in danger from his own countrymen, in danger in the city, in danger in the country, in danger at sea, and in danger from false brothers. He labored and toiled and often gone without sleep, without food. He was cold and naked.

Clearly, Paul had suffered greatly for the Gospel. However, God used those circumstances to make Paul more mature and to give him a great love for God and for spreading God's Word. Those times of testing allowed Paul to grow closer to God, qualifying him to be a great witness for Christ. Even though Paul had these challenges, he was not moved by them.

So, if you are going through a difficult time in your life; you were tested positive for COVID-19, you lost your job, you are experiencing financial challenges, or you're overwhelmed by the political climate and social injustice, rest assured that God will restore and renew your hope in Him. God wants to bless you with a future of faith and love. Continue to trust His promises, He will grant you the desires of your heart according to His will.

Therefore, don't always beg God to change your circumstances. Instead, view each as an opportunity for God to change you, making you mature and complete, not lacking anything.

The hardships we experience in our lives, is nothing compared to the wonderful home the Lord prepared for us. Let's use these hardship experiences to draw closer to God. He is willing and able to help us overcome these hardships.

Oh, Heavenly Father, how thankful we are to have a Savior who looks out for our best interest. Increase our faith, help us to trust You more, help us to stop worry about the hardships we experience and place our trust in You. Help us to find time to sit at your feet, help us to pray without ceasing. Give us an obedient Spirit to respond to Your Word. In times of uncertainty, let our faith be larger than a mustard seed. Help us to trust in You daily knowing that You know what is best for us. We are relying on

your mercies and ever-flowing grace. Let us Not be Moved by our problems, challenges, trials, hardships, but may we stand firm on Your Word. Amen!

Dr. Donna Barrett

Hope

But those who hope in the Lord will renew their strength. They will soar on wings like eagles; they will run and not grow weary; they will walk and not be faint. Isaiah 40:31

Have you ever felt like it's all over and your life is a complete failure? Life appears to be just passing you by and try as you may you never get a fair share of anything. Everyone else seems to be okay but not you. Something is missing and you feel that if you can achieve it, then you will be fine like everyone else. But you take a closer look at their faces, and you see hurt, pain, disappointment, and anxiety. So now you really feel like quitting but don't, because there is someone who is able to help you to succeed. Let me introduce him to you:

I give you Jesus

When you are weary, troubled, or depressed

When your everyday life is filled with stress

When everything seems like a great big mess, I give you Jesus

I give you Jesus

When the ones you love have left you alone

When all you can do is grieve, cry, and mourn

When there's nothing in this world that you can call your own, I give you Jesus

I give you Jesus

When nothing in your life seems to be going right

When hope is like a shadow passing in the night

When there seems to be no relief ever in sight, I give you Jesus

I give you Jesus each and every day

I give you Jesus every step of the way

I give you Jesus till the coming judgment day

Friend, please accept my Jesus

When you do, your heart will be filled with joy unspeakable and a peace that passeth all understanding. He will take away your heavy burdens if you let him and renew your strength like the eagle's. Really, HE is our only Hope.

Our Father in Heaven, thank You for the wonderful promise that You gave us that when we cast our burdens upon You, You

will take care of us. Thank You for the sacrifice of Your son Jesus which guarantees Your faithfulness to us. Amen.

Sharon Roberts

God's Amazing Grace

"Therefore, brethren, having boldness to enter the Holiest by the blood of Jesus." Heb. 10:19

Grace is the source of our salvation. It is also the motive for living the Christian life. God's amazing grace is the guarantee of our salvation. This is a wonderful truth. Some people believe in getting saved by grace and staying saved by works. That's patently impossible. What God starts; he finishes. We are not saved because we hold onto God's hand but only because his almighty hand holds onto our tiny hand. He holds us, we don't hold him.

Grace found us, grace will keep us, grace will not let us go. Those whom God saves; He saves forever. Not one of God's children will ever be lost. All his sheep will eventually find their way home to Heaven. God's grace is truly the heart of the Christian faith and the sum of our message. It is the beginning, middle and end of the Christian life. We are saved by grace, kept by grace, taken to Heaven by grace, and throughout eternity "we've no less days to sing His praise than when we've first begun." Grace is God's gift to you. But a gift must be received in order to be enjoyed. Through grace you can belong to Jesus not for the years of time alone, but for eternity.

May the amazing grace of God continue to redeem, restore and encourage you on your Christian journey. My prayer is that you will experience God's amazing grace in a new way. Remember God loves you! His amazing grace is reaching out to you offering you abundant life for today- a life that will last through eternity. Today if you hear His voice harden not your heart

May God's Amazing Grace ever be Your guide. May God bless and keep You! Amen!

God Opens a Great Door in Paris

"...Behold, I have set before thee an open door, and no man can shut it:" Revelation 3:8

I suffer with a chronic cough that I can trace back to the days when I was a Montessori teacher in Saint Cloud, a chic Parisian suburb. My students were so attached to me that even when they had colds and coughs, they insisted on coming to school. As a result, my immune system was compromised, and I never took the time to properly recover.

Fast forward, years later March 2020, the French president Emmanuel Macron in an address to the nation announced the most stringent measures to combat the pandemic. He announced a total lockdown of the country. Schools, businesses, art museums, parks, cafes, everything would be closed until they could flatten the curve of the virus. No one could leave their place of abode unless they were essential workers. We were given a day and a half to prepare. My son Andrew and I stood for hours in a long line to shop. It was a tense time as shoppers scrambled to buy toilet paper, bottled water, any and every food item they could get their hands on. It was amazing to see how just yesterday the supermarkets were brimming over with all kinds of foods and now store shelves were almost empty.

The confinement, as the French referred to it, was great on one level because we got to spend time together as a family. On the other hand, it posed a serious threat to my health because I could not leave our apartment to take my daily promenades. My well-being depended on it. Confinement was strictly enforced, and you were not allowed to exercise beyond a half mile radius of your neighborhood. If you didn't have a written justification for being outside you risked paying a heavy fine. This confinement was reminiscent of the days when Nazi Germany briefly seized power in France.

Week One of the lockdown: I had a prolong coughing attack, then I knew it was time to leave Paris and return to my tranquil suburban home in Alabama. How could I leave? It was now too late. Macron had just days ago announced that continental Europe would close their borders, and no one could leave or enter Europe. The press reported that thousands of Americans were stranded overseas without any way to return home.

The American Embassy, for weeks, had been advising Americans and its permanent residents to leave the French territory due to the COVID-19 threat but we had decided to stay because we had lived through so many French crisis. The bitter prolonged labor strikes between the government and the unions, the fiery protest of the Gilet Jaune (Yellow Vests), and the burning of Notre Dame. I thought this too would pass and things would soon return to normal.

Early Sabbath morning during my personal time with God, He distinctly spoke to me, "Stephanie, it is time to leave Paris!" But, I said, "how Lord can I leave Paris, the borders are closed, and no one can enter or leave Europe? I don't have any choice but to stay. I thought, "God can put a protective hedge around me in Paris." I didn't want to leave because I knew that the love of my life, my husband Gill, would have to remain to manage his law firm. The thought of leaving him alone in Paris was just too much for me.

The following day, my cough worsened. My husband was alarmed. Our son Kevin, living in Montreal called daily to get an update on my health. Andrew said, *"Mom you must leave France. I will check the US Embassy website to see when we can get a flight to America."* (Notice his faith, he said 'when' and not 'if') By that time, I had been shut up in our apartment for more than a week and deprived of my afternoon walks along the Seine River. It had taken a toll on my health. I was a certain candidate for the Coronavirus, and death stared me in the face.

As I was thinking, my son burst into my room with a big smile on his face and said, "Mom, we can leave on Friday in five days!" "Thank You Lord!" I exclaimed. "But the tickets must cost a fortune on such a short notice?" "No," he explained, "I went on the American Embassy website and a tweet was posted that said that Air France in collaboration with the American government were offering two daily flights from Paris/New York and Paris/LAX for American citizens and its permanent residents."

It was a miracle! First, the tickets were affordable. Secondly, the United States government had completely closed its borders and now it was allowing flights from France to enter America. I knew God had personally intervened on my behalf and allowed the presidents of France and the United States to change their policy just for me! (Read Daniel 10)

We immediately went on Air France website to purchase the tickets, a transaction that would normally take only minutes evolved into a six-hour ordeal because our bank repeatedly flagged our purchase as fraud. Each time we had to call the bank to assure them that we were in Paris and had authorized the purchase of the tickets. The restriction was lifted after each call, only for another uninformed fraud specialist to block our account. Finally, my son recommended that we use PayPal. In a matter of minutes, we had our tickets!

We now had our tickets but how could we get to the airport? The French government had all but shut down public and private transportation limiting its access to essential workers. Anyone without proof or justification would be heavily fined. God inspired my husband to call our friend Hugues, a taxi driver, to take us. The road to the airport was never so short. The highway was deserted. We arrived at record time.

The sprawling, bustling Charles de Gaulle Airport was empty, except for several hundred Americans and the airport personnel. It was at this moment that I saw the omnipotence of God. Who but God could open a continent, a nation, an airport that was under lockdown by a European Union decree? "Ask of Me, and I will give you the nations for your inheritance, and the ends of the earth for your possession." Psalm 2:8 NKJV.

We arrived in the US safe and sound and Coronavirus free.

Prayer for Today: O Lord, when I am confronted with the impossible, help me to remember that You are Alpha and Omega, the beginning and the end. You are omnipotent, omniscient, and never overwhelmed by a situation or caught off guard. There is no door shut in my life, that at Your command, You cannot open because you love me. Amen!

Stephanie Johnson-Dingome

A Heart To Forgive

When I was asked to write this testimonial, I kept asking the LORD what I can write about, what can I say, how can I write on one topic, when I've experience you in every area. As a little girl my father would wake us up at 5a.m. every morning to pray and read the Bible. At the age of (12) at a Sunday morning service I went up during altar call and asked the Lord to save me. It wasn't an easy road. So, I would pray and ask Jesus to give me a heart like His, a heart to love unconditionally, a heart to forgive others in spite of whatever anyone has done to me, help me to forgive and move on. I went through being treated like I didn't belong and was not a part of the family. I was sexually abused by friends of the family and so I started running away from home thinking it would be better if I was out of the reach of these people, however, I ran into the hands of other people who sexually abused me.

There were times I thought I would lose my mind. So, I started quoting a verse from the Bible. *"This Too Shall Pass."* So every time I felt lost or pain or unloved, rejected by the people I thought should love me, I would start to cry in my alone spot or go in the bathroom while taking a shower, so no one would hear or see me cry, and with tears and water running down my face I would say, "*This Too Shall Pass.*" Subsequently, I got married and believed it would all be better now, but the abuse just changed hands. No, my husband never hit me, sometimes I wished he would have. But the mental, verbal, and psychological abuse, the rejection and the neglect was killing me slowly on the inside. But no one saw it; I wore it well. No one noticed it.

After I got saved, I served in different ministries, youth choir, youth leader, youth director, sanctuary choir, and prayer team leader assistant. Instead of focusing on myself and what I was going through, I would hold Bible Studies and prayer sessions after school in my parent's front room with my nieces, nephews and the neighbor's children. I didn't know what I was doing at the time, I just thought it was a good thing to do and as soon as I learned something about God I would teach them. All my life, even in marriage, I kept assisting in the Ministry, I wore a mask, hurting, crying on the inside, went through separation for (2) two years from my husband, lost my home, my business, my mother all at once and then almost lost my mind. Can't they hear me? When family or friends called, I would drop everything to encourage and minister to their needs and put myself on the back because I felt I didn't matter. Also, I didn't understand the same God who love the people He sent me to also love me now some time's I think now He loves me just a little bit more. LOL. Why? He thought me how to truly love myself how to appreciate this woman He made me to be and how to forgive myself for me to forgive others that I can truly be forgiven by Him. His love is so amazing.

No matter what I went through even when I walked away from ministry and didn't want to serve, He loved me in spite of it until I go back to serving Him. I've been serving Him ever since. Now, today my husband is saved and we're back together, I'm serving in ministry in prayer as the SPIRIT OF GOD leads and our businesses have been restored. Forgiveness is not for others, it is for you, that your soul can find rest and peace in the HOLY GHOST, so that you can be effective in the work God has called you to do.

Heavenly FATHER I give You the praise, the honor and all the glory because it all belongs to you. LORD I pray for the person reading this and I ask that Jehovah Rapha, the GOD that heals, heal them everywhere they hurt. LORD you are a heart fixer and there's nothing to hard for You to do. LORD keep them in perfect peace as their minds are stayed on You. LORD JESUS help them to see You in the midst of every trial and the good times. It is written, the weapons will form but they shall not prosper FATHER GOD, You are the restorer according to Your Word LORD GOD restore everything, the locust, the cankerworm, the caterpillar and the palmerworm have stolen. Grant them Your divine favor, Your grace and Your mercy LORD GOD in no other name but the LORD JESUS CHRIST. Amen!

Shantell N.L. Florival

Trusting God Through It All!

"A thousand may fall at your side, ten thousand at your right hand, but it will not come near you." Psalm 91:7

Covid-19! Nothing else needs to be said about this name. This is a deadly pestilence that has stalks us in the darkness and has disturb our life in 2020. We have seen thousands fall at our side and ten thousand at our right hand, but the Lord declares that it will not come near my dwelling place nor my families' dwelling place. Psalms 91, my daily repetition of this Psalms has carried me through to this day. Believing in the word of God and trusting Him daily to protect my family as we go out and come in. Knowing that God is my refuge and my dwelling place where I can run to for protection, understanding that He has discharged my angels to encamped around me and my family through it all.

During this unprecedented time in our world, we are told by God not to fear but to trust Him, not to lean on our own understanding, because we sure do not understand Covid-19. But, in all our ways we are to acknowledge God for His goodness, and His grace, and mercies that He grants us every morning. We are to thank Him for His daily protection and blessings He gives us, not to succumb to this dangerous disease that is circulating around us.

So, it is with a thankful and grateful heart I continue to trust my Lord through is all, meditating on His promises and calling upon Him to be my Rock. I know that Christ the Rock of my salvation is the only place to be anchored in during these times. I trust and believe in His covenant to always be at my defense in times of trouble, so I am assured that my families and I will survive and thrive in this pandemic, because we are, "Trusting God through it all."

Heavenly Father, what a friend we have in Jesus all our sins and griefs to bear. Father, I trust in all the promises that You declared over my life that You will not leave nor forsake me, I am trusting You today for divine guidance and protection over my family also as we trust You for our daily bread as well as opportunities You will put in our paths today Lord. Go before us father and make every crooked path straight, in the mighty name of Jesus. Amen!

Susan Gooding-Liburd

Hope

"But let us who are of the day, be sober, putting on the breastplate of faith and love; and for a helmet the hope of salvation." 1 Thess. 5:8

Hope is to live daily exuding confidence, knowing that God has you covered by His blood, protected under His wings and safely nestled in the palm of His hand. Hope is the reinforced fortified belief that God will supply all your needs according to His riches in glory. Hope displays a positive disposition, regardless of which way life's curve ball is thrown at you. It is the final settlement in the mind and the ability to say like the famous song writer, Horatio Spafford, "It is well with my soul."

The year 2012 was a death tsunami for my family. My sister, Hope died in January, my mother died in March and three cousins died In September, October, and December of that year. The deaths left me with more questions than I had answers. I wanted to know where was my faith, hope and most of all my God? I looked deep within my soul, I agonized with God to take away the awful pain I was feeling due to this incredible devastating loss. I searched the Scriptures looking for comfort, then I remembered my mother's last words before she died. She said "Faith, we seen the gleams of the golden morning piercing through this night of gloom. We see the gleams of the golden morning Jesus is coming soon."

I suddenly realized that I had found my strength and comfort. In 1 Thessalonians 4:13-17, "We do not weep as those who have no hope. We know that Jesus died and rose again and will bring to life those who fell asleep in Him. For the dead in Christ shall rise first and we who are alive will be caught up to meet Him in the air, comfort ye one another with these words." I have the blessed hope and assurance of Christ's return. I have the faith to know my hope is built on nothing else than Jesus' blood and righteousness. I have God, who created the universe and is big enough to rule the world yet small enough to dwell within my heart. He comforts, cheers, and guides me providing me with strength and hope to face another day. I have put all my trust in Him and hope for better days to come. I have fortified myself in the belief of reunification with my deceased family members at His second coming. I have noted that God has healed me as time passes by. The pain is not as deep, the wound has closed but it has left a permanent scar behind. However, this reminds that God himself is the blessed hope, who never left me but lovingly guided me all the way through in my lonely hours of pain and despair.

Dear Father, please have mercy on me and help thou my unbelief in my times of weakness. Give me the courage and strength to stay on the ship that You are steering as I put my trust in You. You are the Captain that never fails!

Faith D. Housen

What Would Jesus Do?

And the* LORD *said unto Cain, where is Able thy brother? And he said, I know not: Am I my brother's keeper? And he said, what hast thou done? the voice of thy brother's blood crieth unto me from the ground. ---Genesis 4:9-10

What would Jesus do? This is the question we as Christians should ask ourselves? Should I speak out against the evil tide of racism and violence that has swept across America? Or should I sit quietly by and await the second coming of Christ to end the social evils? Should I pray for peace and let social activists deal with the issues? Should I flee the cities and leave the urban poor and oppressed to their fate? What can one person do? Didn't the Bible predict at the end of time chaos and confusion? Is it my role to work against the fulfillment of prophecy?

Today, more than ever with the murder of George Floyd, Breonna Taylor, Ahmaud Marbery, and the senseless shooting of Jacob Blake, we as Adventists believers need to become our brother's keeper. We must become the Good Samaritan. We cannot pass on the other side while our brothers and sisters are being suffocated in airtight cages of poverty and despair. We must help illegal aliens. Is there any justifiable reason that families should be separated because they don't have a green card? What would Jesus do?

Jesus Our Example

1) He Was a Kind and Compassionate Savior (Matthew 15:30-31)

30 And great multitudes came unto him, having with them those that were lame, blind, dumb, maimed, and many others, and cast them down at Jesus' feet; and he healed them:

31 Insomuch that the multitude wondered, when they saw the dumb to speak, the maimed to be whole, the lame to walk, and the blind to see: and they glorified the God of Israel.

2) He Cared for the Physical Needs of the People (Mark 6: 34-44, Matthew 15:32-38)

34 And Jesus, when he came out, saw many people, and was moved with compassion toward them, because they were as sheep not having a shepherd: and he began to teach them many things.

35 And when the day was now far spent, his disciples came unto him, and said, "This is a desert place, and now the time is far passed."

36 Send them away, that they may go into the country round about, and into the villages, and buy themselves bread: for they have nothing to eat.

37 He answered and said unto them, "Give ye them to eat. And they say unto him, "shall we go and buy two hundred pennyworth of bread, and give them to eat?"

38 He saith unto them, "How many loaves have ye? go and see. And when they knew, they say, Five, and two fishes."

39 And he commanded them to make all sit down by companies upon the green grass.

40 And they sat down in ranks, by hundreds, and by fifties.

41 And when he had taken the five loaves and the two fishes, he looked up to heaven, and blessed, and brake the loaves, and gave them to his disciples to set before them; and the two fishes divided he among them all.

42 And they did all eat and were filled.

43 And they took up twelve baskets full of the fragments, and of the fishes.

44 And they that did eat of the loaves were about five thousand men.

3) He Reached Out to the Migrant, Alien, Outcast (Matthew 15:21-28, Mark 7:24-37)

21 Then Jesus went thence and departed into the coasts of Tyre and Sidon.

22 And, behold, a woman of Canaan came out of the same coasts, and cried unto him, saying, "have mercy on me, O Lord, thou son of David; my daughter is grievously vexed with a devil."

23 But he answered her not a word. And his disciples came and besought him, saying, Send her away; for she crieth after us.

24 But he answered and said," I am not sent but unto the lost sheep of the house of Israel."

25 Then came she and worshipped him, saying, "Lord, help me."

26 But he answered and said, "It is not meet to take the children's bread, and to cast it to dogs."

27 And she said, "Truth, Lord: yet the dogs eat of the crumbs which fall from their masters' table."

[28] Then Jesus answered and said unto her, "O woman, great is thy faith: be it unto thee even as thou wilt. And her daughter was made whole from that very hour."

4) He Didn't Brand People with a Scarlett Letter (Luke 7:36-50, John 4, John 8: 3-11)

[36] And one of the Pharisees desired him that he would eat with him. And he went into the Pharisee's house, and sat down to meat.

[37] And, behold, a woman in the city, which was a sinner, when she knew that Jesus sat at meat in the Pharisee's house, brought an alabaster box of ointment,

[38] And stood at his feet behind him weeping, and began to wash his feet with tears, and did wipe them with the hairs of her head, and kissed his feet, and anointed them with the ointment.

[39] Now when the Pharisee which had bidden him saw it, he spake within himself, saying, "This man, if he were a prophet, would have known who and what manner of woman this is that toucheth him: for she is a sinner."

[40] And Jesus answering said unto him, "Simon, I have somewhat to say unto thee." And he saith, "Master, say on."

41 There was a certain creditor which had two debtors: the one owed five hundred pence, and the other fifty.

42 And when they had nothing to pay, he frankly forgave them both. Tell me therefore, which of them will love him most?

43 Simon answered and said, “I suppose that he, to whom he forgave most. And he said unto him, thou hast rightly judged.”

44 And he turned to the woman, and said unto Simon, “Seest thou this woman? I entered into thine house, thou gavest me no water for my feet: but she hath washed my feet with tears and wiped them with the hairs of her head.”

45 Thou gavest me no kiss, but this woman since the time I came in hath not ceased to kiss my feet.

46 My head with oil thou didst not anoint, but this woman hath anointed my feet with ointment.

47 Wherefore I say unto thee, “Her sins, which are many, are forgiven; for she loved much: but to whom little is forgiven, the same loveth little.”

48 And he said unto her, “Thy sins are forgiven.”

49 And they that sat at meat with him began to say within themselves, “Who is this that forgiveth sins also?”

50 And he said to the woman, “Thy faith hath saved thee; go in peace.”

5) He Loved Families and Celebrated Children (Matthew 19:14)

14 But Jesus said, "suffer little children, and forbid them not, to come unto me: for of such is the kingdom of heaven".

6) He Took A Strong Stand Against Exploitation and Greed (John 2:13-17)

13 And the Jews' Passover was at hand, and Jesus went up to Jerusalem.

14 And found in the temple those that sold oxen and sheep and doves, and the changers of money sitting:

15 And when he had made a scourge of small cords, he drove them all out of the temple, and the sheep, and the oxen; and poured out the changers' money and overthrew the tables.

16 And said unto them that sold doves, "Take these things; hence, make not my Father's house an house of merchandise."

17 And his disciples remembered that it was written, the zeal of thine house hath eaten me up.

7) He Made Disciples of Ordinary Men

[19] And he saith unto them, "Follow me, and I will make you fishers of men."

[20] And they straightway left their nets and followed him.

Now I ask you as a follower of Christ," what will you do to make a difference?"

Today's Prayer: Lord make me like Jesus. Give me Your Spirit so that I might have the courage to stand up, speak out, and lovingly care for the oppressed and those who have no might. Amen

Stephanie Johnson-Dingome

God Is Forgiving and Merciful

The Lord our God is merciful and forgiving, even though we have rebelled against Him Daniel 9:9

The ending of July 2016 hit me like a ton of brick. I lost my Papa (grandfather) and my husband, and I separated. I was numb, lost, broken, and confused. It felt like my entire world collapsed before me. I asked God how this could be, why me. Anger, bitterness, hurt, pain, rejection, and resentment filled my heart. I told myself that I deserve to be happy, so I set off to do just that, or so I thought. I began partying and "living my best life" which pushed me further away from what I needed which was more of God. Doors were opened that shouldn't have been opened and relationships formed that shouldn't have beenfor me.

I'm finally free and happy!!! Then I heard the voice of the Lord saying to me there's healing in my presence, there's peace in my presence, this is not my will for you, I fell on my face and wept. What have I done, the one person who never left me was the one I walked away from? The relationship ended and the doors were closed. As I reflected on all the things, I'd done I felt ashamed and felt as if I'd let both myself and God down, but I remembered how merciful God is. On my face I repented, I forgave those who hurt me, and I forgave myself.

Lord, I thank You for being a forgiving and merciful God, I thank You for mending the broken pieces of my heart. I thank You for the truth of Your word that will always guide me to do the right thing and even if I do wrong, I know that once I ask for forgiveness, I will receive it. Amen!

Crystal Dames

Hope

"For I know the plans I have for you, declares the Lord, plans to prosper you and not to harm you, plans to give you hope and a future." Jer. 29:11

God knows that we all struggle and lose hope when facing some situations. Everyone needs encouragement when facing tests of our faith from time to time.

For as long as I can recall the months of March and August represented a "dip" into valleys of despair as I traversed through my life's journey. It seems that there was period during the year when significant challenges would always surface in my life. First, it was March madness followed by the perennial August surprise. Once I was able to recognize this pattern, I began to pray to the Lord for the strength to overcome these cyclic periods of transit into these valleys of despair. So instead of temporarily moving into the valley, I prayed to enjoy seasons of blessings. While I began to experience favorable relief during March, I was still encountering the August surprise because it seems that I was only faintly hoping for change.

In reflection over my life's journey with my husband, he pointed out to me that March madness no longer presented any difficulty because I had imbued my faith by adopting an abundant blessing mindset. By leaning on the Lord to provide for my needs and equip me with unlimited blessings to address whatever may come my way, I had successfully exited the March valley. However, I still had anxiety about the looming August surprises because I had not used my faith to conquer my fears.

This situation was put to the test when the Covid19 pandemic began to ravish our world. As we went into lock down in March, I did not have any anxiety because my faith was strong that this too shall pass. I didn't have a ticket stamped for the destination to the March madness valley. When family and friends began to fall into despair, I became their cheerleader and coach. I was able to provide guidance for many of them opening their eyes to a plethora of opportunities that promoted new seasons of abundance for them. Some started new thriving businesses and others were able to pivot and take better control of their world. I set up a series of virtual conferences targeting at-risk communities and providing information to help save lives and promote wellness. I had turned lemon into lemon aide.

Pressing forward with August looming on the horizon, I knew my own personal test was ahead. This year I would really need to lean heavily on the Lord to overcome my new valley, unemployment. Still unsure about how I would land on my feet after the difficult few years that I had encountered with my former employer. I had finally separated at year end because it was clear that my services were no longer needed nor was there any support to retain me. In fact, I was strongly encouraged by a leader in the Big Four consulting firm to go where I would be appreciated and celebrated and not just tolerated.

This journey to secure new employment began you guessed it in August 2019. So, now amid a global pandemic, I anxiously watched my savings dwindle away. It was time for the big test. Here I am Lord awaiting this season's favor of the August surprise. In this season, more than ever I desperately needed this situation turned around. My family was depending on me to resolve the cash flow problem and keep a roof over our heads. It was essential for me to achieve the end result. I had high "hope" that 2020 would be the year that I would finally conquer my August demon.

After a full year of soliciting job leads from colleagues and friends, scrolling through job boards, answering solicitations from random recruiters, submitting hundreds of applications and powering through dozens of interviews, I watched the days on the calendar lapse as the clock toll towards August. Something was different. Somehow, I knew that this year I would finally score a victory over August. My "hope" for a different outcome grew more and more fervent because I now had hope combined with the faith of a mustard seed that my valley would soon be behind me.

My prayer was answered in the blink of an eye when I received a message that the position that I had applied for last August was finally being cleared to hire and I was selected as the candidate to fill the position. On the last Friday evening in July, the hiring manager reached out to me and cut through all the red tape to ensure that my start date would be the first business day of the new month. I was told to report for duty on August 3rd!

My prayers were answered in abundance. My offer came through -the contract was fully funded for a year and I can work from the comfort of my home and I received a significant salary increase. I am now well positioned to successfully navigate any August surprise. I was put into a place where my presence is appreciated, and my contributions celebrated. Even during a pandemic, the Lord had elevated me and shown me great favor. Doors were opened that no one can close. I was able to see how "hope" can be manifested and prayers answered.

According to the scriptures, "no good thing does the Lord withhold from those that walk uprightly" (Psalm 84:11) As David prayed in the Psalm 18:2." The Lord is my rock, my fortress and my deliverer; my God is my rock, in whom I take refuge, my shield and the horn of my salvation, my stronghold." I call upon the Lord, who is worthy to be praised, and I am saved." (Psalm 18:19) He bought me out into a broad place; he rescued me, because he delighted in me."

Dear Lord, help us to be encouraged despite how it may look through your eyes. We call on You Lord to lift us up out of the "strife" and ...show steadfast love to Your anointed. Amen!

Claudette Johnson

His Purpose for My Life

I have been young, and now am old; yet have I not seen the Righteous forsaken nor his seed begging bread. Psalm 37:24

God's purpose for my life is to develop a deep sincere trusting relationship with Him, where He is seen as a Father who protects, provides, counsels, and guides me in my daily life. In response to His goodness towards me, I will trust and obey His word. I will submit my will to His will without doubt, I will forever lean upon His everlasting arms; knowing his grace is sufficient to carry me through the uncertain journey of life, preparing me for His second coming to dwell with Him forever more.

In contemplation of God's purpose for my life, I studied the lives of certain individuals in the Bible, who have left an indelible impression on society from they were children into adulthood until the day they died. Although they are no longer with us, their principled lives and positive character traits remain behind and still live on. They were not perfect human beings, but their lifestyle serves as a model in successfully knowing God's purpose for my life.

Moses was placed in a basket among the bulrushes by his mother, to escape certain death which had been ordered by Pharaoh of Egypt. When he became of age, he served God until his death.

Joshua was a young man from the twelve tribes of Israel. He too purposed in his heart to serve God and became the successor to Moses in leading the children of Israel. Samuel was dedicated to the Lord as a child by his mother, he was under the tutelage of Eli, the Priest in the temple. He was one of the most revered Old Testament Prophets in his day who faithfully served the Lord until he was translated up to heaven. David, the second known King of Israel who determined in his heart at a young age to serve God no matter the cost. He was a king who fought and won many battles under God's guidance for the children of Israel. He is the author of many of our beloved psalms, which at times reflected the uncomfortable fearful situations he faced. The only solution for him, was to request help from his creator, the Almighty God.

In reviewing the lives of these Bible Characters, I found out the common factors which made them have a successful purpose in life and I intend to follow and apply them in principle to knowing God's purpose for my life. Moses, Joshua, Samuel, and David exhibited determination, strength, and fortitude. They were obedient to God and trusted in his word without vacillation. They displayed a humble disposition and were kind to their fellow men. They acquired knowledge through daily communication with God and applied and used it wisely. They praised, blessed, and thanked God for his continual presence and goodness in their lives.

I pray dear God that as I present myself to You to be used as an instrument of your vessel; I will be molded and fashioned after Your will. I will trust, follow, and obey Your word in order to become more like You in developing the mental acumen in knowing Your purpose for my life. Amen!

Faith D. Housen

The God who Supersedes Safe

He was in the lower part of the ship, asleep on a pillow: and they awake him, and say unto him, Master, carest thou not that we perish? And he arose and rebuked the wind and said unto the sea, "Peace, be still." And the wind ceased, and there was a great calm. And he said unto them "Why are ye so fearful? How is it that ye have no faith?" And they feared exceedingly, and said one to another, "What manner of man is this, that even the wind and the sea obey him?" Mark 4:38-41

Have you ever been in a situation that no matter how you look at it, the end result is most dire? I am sure we can each think of a situation that makes our heart palpitate much harder than it should, and we wish we could go back to sleep and wake up somewhere else. Whatever the reason, we feel that God has let us down. He is in the bottom of the boat, asleep, while we have to walk the hard road alone. "Does he even care?"

These are times when blind faith is what is really needed. We must know that "He cares," even if He doesn't answer like we want Him to. He loves us far too much to leave us alone. The pain may be unbearable, but He is still in control. He still says "Peace, be still, why are you so fearful? Have you no faith?" Truth be told, we want to have faith, but facts are staring us straight in the face, and we can't get around it. Yet He still says "Peace, be still." If we will open our spiritual eyes, and see that this is the God of the universe, inviting us to put our hands in His, and trust Him, blindly take a step of faith, may not we ask, "what manner of man is this?"

We want that safe God. We want to know that the story ends well. But what if it doesn't? Really, is that the end?

C.S. Lewis in "The Lion, the Witch and the Wardrobe", gives us an insight into the truth, when Mr. Beaver gave his answer to Susan, relating to Aslan the Lion (a picture of God): *"Aslan is a lion- the Lion, the great Lion." "Ooh" said Susan. "I'd thought he was a man. Is he quite safe? I shall feel rather nervous about meeting a lion." ...safe? said Mr. Beaver... "Who said anything about safe? 'course he isn't safe. But he's good. He's the king, I tell you.'*

God is beyond safe. He is omniscient! He knows the full story from the end right back to the beginning. He knows what road will bring us where; and so, He says "Peace, be still - know I Am God." What do we have to lose? We are already at the bottom anyway. Should we take the leap of faith and fully trust Him, will we be like Daniel - the morning after his night with the lions? (*see Daniel 6:16-23*).

Our story does not end here. Our challenge is to jump in at the deep end, trust in His peace, trust in His care. Let's take the challenge and jump in with the God who supersedes safe. May we be able to give a report of the message that results from our messes. May we be able to say for ourselves "What manner of man is this."

Dear Father God, thank You for knowing what is best for us. Our choice is to be delivered from the trials we face from day to day, and we know You are more than able to deliver us, but even if You choose instead, to walk with us through these trials, we are thankful. We are thankful because we know Your way is the best way. We are thankful because we know You care, and You ask us to be still and know You are God. Help us to realize when we come to the end of our story, that You are not just a safe God, but you are way beyond awesome. You deliver us in amazing ways. May we like the disciples realize and say, "what manner of man is this." All these we pray in Jesus' name.

Viviene Davis

Fear Thou Not for I Am with Thee

Be careful for nothing; but in everything by prayer and supplication with thanksgiving let your requests be made known unto God. And the peace of God, which passeth all understanding, shall keep your hearts and minds through Christ Jesus. Phil. 4:6-7

I grew up a Seventh-day Adventist and I am always a strong believer in the power of prayer, but I had a weakness. I had a fear of anesthesia and surgery and even worst the big C. I would always say to myself I would never want to hear that I needed to undergo a surgery, which is also associated with anesthesia or that I have cancer. Many friends and family refer to me as a health freak, because I am very cautious of my diet and exercise, so I was so sure I was very healthy.

In Nov of 2018 I had an appointment with my gynecologist and was told there was a lump in my breast, and a mammogram was urgent. Three months later I did the mammogram, next a biopsy was requested, which was diagnosed that I had breast cancer. To make matters worse, less than a week after my diagnosis I was in a car accident where I clearly saw my death, but I came out without a scratch.

I encountered my fear in March 2019 because I had my first surgery a lumpectomy and was convinced that was it. To my surprise my surgeon saith he was not satisfied so I would need to do a mastectomy. Two weeks later I had the mastectomy and a reconstruction of the breast. The rest of 2019 I had chemotherapy every six week, today I can say thank you Jesus, you brought me through.

Fear is defined as, a distressing emotion aroused by impending danger, evil, pain, etc., whether the threat is real or imagined; the feeling or condition of being afraid. a specific instance of or propensity for such a feeling: an abnormal fear of heights, concern or anxiety; solicitude: a fear for someone or something.

My fears were encountered in 2019, but my fear of the Lord was also strengthened. My prayer life was on high. Jesus was my doctor, my surgeon, my healer, and my deliverer and today, He is still working on me. Today, I overcame my fears by depending upon the word of God. Fears can be powerful and can take control of one's life.

Isaiah 41:10 says, "Fear thou not; for I am with thee: be not dismayed; for I am thy God: I will strengthen thee; yea, I will help thee; yea, I will uphold thee with the right hand of my righteousness."

Our Heavenly Father told us not to fear because He has our back. We can be confident in His words. I am a witness that He

will never leave us or forsake us. Yes, 2019 was a real struggle for me, but with it all I was not afraid, I learned to totally depend on Jesus, and you can too. Amen!

Marcia Powell

Note to Self

"For all have sinned and fall short of the Glory of God" Romans 3:23

I often hear the phrase "Note to Self." I have even used it as hashtags on social media posts and said it when thinking of something I want to make sure I remember. When I started to think about what "Note to Self" really means I realized that it's a reminder - A reminder to ourselves. What do you need to remind yourself? For some it's a reminder on how to lose weight, or a reminder to eat healthier or maybe it's a note to self to take time for self-care. There are many "things" we can remind ourselves but one I want to take a minute to share with you could make all the difference in your outlook on like. "Note to Self" – Forgive Yourself! It sounds easy right? Forgive yourself! Yes! Forgive Yourself!

Forgiveness is hard. It's hard to forgive others but if you are like me, it's even harder to forgive yourself. You may have heard that forgiveness is not for the other person but instead it's for you. I would also add that it's even more important after forgiving other that you understand the important of forgiving yourself and that is for you. It's one of the hardest things you must do in your journey to growth and peace. Forgive yourself for your peace of mind. I struggled for years with forgiving myself for mistakes I made. For loving too hard or for not leaving sooner or not setting the boundaries that protected my peace; there were so many reasons I needed to forgive myself. I found that because I hadn't forgiven myself, I spent a lot of time listening to my negative thoughts and judging myself hard. So, Note to Self...Forgive Yourself! Stop punishing yourself! Stop blaming yourself! I was a hostage to my past as I was constantly reviewing and reliving my mistakes. I would replay certain events and I felt like I was living with regrets. It's time to stop the "video player" in your mind. Stop reminding yourself of what should have been, could have been or would have been. If this is you, I pray that this message motivates you to move forward and turn your pain into peace.

So how did I do it? How can you? How do you forgive yourself? The first step towards forgiving yourself is to focus on accepting the mistakes you made. Everyone makes mistakes, sometimes they are intentional, but God loves you regardless and in spite of the mistakes you have made. Accept God's love as a reminder that no matter what you have done, He loves you. Remember Romans 3:23 says, "For all have sinned and fall short of the Glory of God." I had to make that scripture a picture on my phone so I would remember that no one is perfect, and God loves me in spite of my mistakes. Another Scripture that I focused on was Psalm 32:5 which says, "I acknowledged my mistakes to you (God), and you forgave them." This Psalm showed me that when I prayed, God forgave me but if I hadn't forgiven myself, then I was still in a state of spiritual bondage. Will you take the first step? Pray and accept the mistakes you made and allow the Word of God to help you to move forward.

The second step is to create affirmations. Some of mine are "I am strong," "I am grateful for my past and the lessons I learned," and "I truly love myself completely." These positive affirmations kept reminding me that although this is hard, I must do this for me. I must change my future by forgiving myself of my past. I wrote the affirmations in my journal and I also created a vision board with my affirmations to keep a visual reminder. Affirmations helped me to change the "video player" in my mind. Try it today…write positive thoughts and affirmations about yourself. Where will you write your affirmations and place them as a reminder? What will you say about yourself? It's not easy but start today.

The third step in the process of forgiving yourself is to release it! What do I mean by releasing it? I released it by writing myself a letter. In the letter, I wrote about my feelings, my regrets, my mistakes, and everything that was keeping me from moving forward. If you are worried about your letter being found, write it, release your feelings, and shred it or throw it away. A friend of mine and I were talking about ways to move past the pain and hurt and when I gave her this advice, she wrote the letter and then burned it. It was very liberating to Release It and Let It Go! Move on!

Today is the day to move forward! To move on! Will you, do it? Will you take the steps towards Forgiving Yourself? Maya Angelou once said "It's one of the greatest gifts you can give yourself, to forgive. Forgive everybody," and I will add that everybody includes You! Take the Steps! Move Forward towards Peace, the Peace that surpasses all understanding. Peace exists! Joy Exists! Happiness Exists! Note to Self - Forgive Yourself!

Father God, I come to You humbly asking You to heal me from the inside out. I know that all have sinned and fall short of Your glory including me. You have forgiven me for my past mistakes and Lord, I now ask that You to open my heart to allow me to forgive myself. I thank You Lord for deliverance from the negative voices that may be playing over and over, from any guilt I have and that I realize that You sent Your Son, Jesus Christ to die on the Cross for me. Increase my faith and may I see myself as You see me, Lord. May I have the freeing Joy and Peace that You promise. This prayer I ask in the matchless name of Jesus Christ. Amen!

Michele Edwards-Collie

Forgiveness

And be kind one to another, tenderhearted, forgiving one another, even as God for Christ sake has forgiven you. Eph 4:32

What is forgiveness and how do you find it your heart to forgive someone who has done you great harm? Forgiveness is defined as the intellectual and voluntary process by which, one undergoes a change in feeling and attitude regarding an offence and to overcome negative emotions such as resentment and vengeance.

Eph 3:32 clearly states that we should forgive one another even as Christ has forgiven us. Sounds very simply, but sometimes it is very difficult to do so. The process of forgiveness cannot be achieved unless we depend on Our Heavenly Father to guide us through, it can only be accomplished through Jesus Christ our Savior our Lord.

Let us remember that all things are possible through Christ. He loves us so much and in so doing He has forgiven us so many times and so we need to extend the same kind of love to our brothers and sisters. Let us not just forgive but also forget and move on. Forgiveness includes forgetting the actions of the accuser. Once you forgive and forget the accuser's actions, you will feel like a burden is lifted from your shoulders. You will feel like a new person in Christ Jesus.

Let us pray that as we live our lives daily, we will learn to forgive others and forget the actions that we are forgiving and as we do so, Jesus Christ will also forgive us of our sins.

Holy Holy Holy! Lord GOD Almighty we love You, we praise Your Holy name. You love us so much that You died on the cross to save us. You have forgiven us so many times over and over. By Your grace we extend the same kind of forgiveness to others as we live our lives daily. We know that this process is impossible without You, so we commit ourselves into Your care because we know all things are possible with You. We thank we bless Your Holy name Amen!

Lorna Keize

Fasting & Praying

Biblical fasting is refraining from food for a spiritual purpose. Fasting has always been a normal part of a relationship with God. As expressed by the impassioned plea of David in Psalm 42, fasting brings one into a deeper, more intimate and powerful relationship with the Lord.

When you eliminate food from your diet for several days, your spirit becomes uncluttered by the things of this world and amazingly sensitive to the things of God. As David stated, Deep calls unto deep" (Psalm 42:7). David was fasting. His hunger and thirst for God were greater than his natural desire for food. As a result, he reached a place where he could cry out from the depths of his spirit to the depths of God, even in the midst of his trial. Once you've experienced even a glimpse of that kind of intimacy with our God - Our Father, the Holy Creator of the universe - and the countless rewards and blessings that follow, your whole perspective will change. You will soon realize that fasting is a secret source of power that is overlooked by many.

Once you make that decision to fast, even if it is just for a day God sees the desires of your heart. He will provide you with the grace to endure and see the breakthrough you need come to pass.

Why Fast and Pray

1. It releases the anointing, the favor and the blessing of God in the life of a Christian.

2. It releases supernatural power - If Jesus could have accomplished all He came to do without fasting, why should He fast? The Son of God fasted because He knew there were supernatural things that could only be released that way. How much more should fasting be a common practice in our lives?

3. Jesus fasted – According to Peter, Jesus is our example in all things (1 Peter 2:21)

4. Fasting and prayer bring you to a place of being able to clearly hear God's will.

Whether you desire to be closer to God or need great breakthroughs in your life, remember that nothing shall be impossible when you pray. Fasting and prayer is truly the secret source of power. Ask, Seek, Knock and Wait for God's blessings to overflow in your life.

Dear Jesus helps us to fast and pray more for the infilling of the Holy Spirit. Only when we are filled with Your Spirit are we able to do supernatural things. Not by might nor by power but by Your Holy Spirit. Teach us to fast and pray. We desire to be more like You in everything that we do. We love and adore you in the Mighty name of Jesus. Amen!

Dr. Donna Barrett

Intercessory Prayers

And it shall come to pass, that before they call, I will answer; and while they are yet speaking, I will hear. Isaiah 65 v. 24.

Spiritual communication between man and God is an important two-way relationship as we not only talk to God but listen to Him. Interceding for ourselves or on behalf of others, we partner with the Spirit of God to accomplish His will. In January 2018, I studied and sat for a state board licensure to acquire state licensure in my professional field of practice. Passing this examination was important as it would open opportunities to afford me a promotion and additional credential. The examination was two parts and successful passing of both sections were necessary to ascertain passing. I paid the exam fee, studied, prayed, and sat the exam which was graded immediately after completion. After submitting my exam, the result returned indicating that I passed one section but failed the other. I was sorely disappointed. Feeling discouraged, I decided not to redo the exam due to the cost associated with re-sitting and dedicated time to study again.

Days later, I prayed and asked God to reveal why I failed, and to give me a sign if it is His will for me to re-sit the exam. In the back of my mind, I could hear a voice saying, 'you will be successful at the next attempt' but I dismissed it. In mid-February, a friend approached me and inquired if I was successful at passing. As I began to discuss my frustration at failing and determined not to re-sit it, my friend encouraged me to re-sit the exam and reminded me that God's plan for His children is to be the head and not the tail. She also talked to me about the benefits of passing this exam, and she offered to pay if I re-sit. She decided to join in interceding to God on my behalf for me to be successful at re-sitting the exam. Reluctantly, I agreed.

I resumed studying, however, while studying this time around, I prayed and interceded with God before and during studies. My friend also interceded on my behalf and paid for me to re-sit the exam. On the day of re-sitting the exam, opposed to feeling nervous, I felt calm and better prepared. Walking into the exam room I reflected that my friend was interceding for me and I also whispered a prayer begging God to allow me to be successful. At the end of the exam, I was elated to see that I passed both sections of the exam. I cried tears of joy! After collecting my results and exiting the building, I quickly called my friend to share the good news but before I could speak, she yelled, "you passed right?" We both offered up a prayer of thanksgiving to God and this reassured me, that in partnering with the Holy Spirit through intercessory prayers for success, the will of God was manifested.

Loving Father in Heaven, we honor and adore You for who You are in and through our lives. Thank You for loving us and giving us a connection with You through Your Holy Spirit to seek Your direction and input in our lives. Help us to continuously seek Your guidance for Your will in our lives and help us to remember to give You the glory and praise due to your most high and holy name we pray, Amen!

Georgia Sinclair, LMSW, ACM-SW, Medical Social Work

Fasting and Praying

"Is it a fast that I have chosen, A day for a man to afflict his soul? Is it to bow down his head like a bulrush, and to spread out sackcloth and ashes? Would you call this a fast, And an acceptable day to the Lord?...." Isaiah 58:5-9

The year was 1967, and the place was England, a quaint little town in the conurbation of middle England, called Dudley. Indeed, England is a place of brilliant essayists, poets, philosophers, able politicians, courageous reformers and renown explorers and legendary lore. Who then was so stout in perception that could have conceived that as a young girl leaving her homeland in Castleton, Jamaica, I would today be writing this testimony?

Perceptibly, the English dramatist and playwright wisely wrote: "All the world is indeed a stage, and all the men and women are simply players." His witty and yet, sober persiflage, Shakespeare provides a profound understanding to my life. Therein, I have found Yahushua to be more than the spider in the web of human affairs, more than the bee in the hive of life's circumstances. He is the honey in the comb that sweetens life's bitterness.

In contrast with the culture's ‘dourness'. The believer should not be taken by moods that are congenially inclined to persiflage and inimical. Any behavior originating in blind conformity to customs and popularity of the world, is often one that meets heaven's disapproval. In other words, Yah, treats us as a priority, therefore, we cannot afford to treat Him as an option! Any attempt to embrace the world and doing violence to one's spirituality, is a step too far.

The words of Thomas Paine, depicting the "American Crisis," are today in a Covid culture, more poignantly relevant than when they were written in 1776. It was then that he wrote:

"These are the times that try men souls. The summer soldiers and the sunshine patriots will, in this crisis, shrink from the service of their country; but he that stands it now deserves the love and thanks of man and woman."

Throughout my experience, there have been times when I had been sequestered by anguish. At such times, prayer led me to the altar of nobler purposes. Too often men and women enlisted in purposes of Yahusha, have been wounded by their own strong will and neglect of prayer. There is none more obvious than Samson, Judges 13, a man distinguished by his proverbial strength. The toll of his indiscretions is documented for our admonition.

In my experience, I have found Yahusha to be much more than the spider in the web of human affairs. He is more than the bee in the hive of life's buzzing circumstances. Rather, He is the honey in the comb that sweetens life's relentless bitterness, from which we are consoled.

Thus, like the Psalmist king David, I declare: "I will lift up mine eyes unto the hills, from whence cometh my help, my help cometh from Yahweh. He will not suffer thy foot to be moved: He that keepeth me will not slumber. Behold, He that keepeth Israel shall neither slumber nor sleep. Yahweh is thy keeper; Elohim is thy shade upon my right hand" (Psalm 121: 1-5).

To illuminate the pragmatism of one's faith, it is necessary to demonstrate that its many manifestations are related to the common scriptural framework of 'fasting and prayer.' These principles are presented, not as unstated arbitrary assumptions, but as tried and tested means by our moral ancestors. The principled believer in Yahusha, must engage in prayer and fasting, as part of the solution to many of life's predicaments. They not only connect us to Yah but serve to improve our own relationship with Yah.

Prayer is not an occasional or random act, rather, it is a permanent attitude before Yahweh! It is the awakening of the conscience by Yah's holiness; the purging of the mind with His Word; the cleansing of imagination by Yah's wisdom; the surrendering of the heart to His love; the doing of His purpose—so that His will in heaven, will be manifested on earth. Such is praying!

From the dawn of man's relationship with his Creator, there has existed in his mind, the need to seek help from this Supreme Celestial source. It finds expression in the tradition of praying and fasting, a submission of the will, to attain rectitude by way of humility before the King. Genuine prayer finds acceptance in Yah's inclined ears, and approval in His nostrils.

I can do no better than to quote one of Yahusha's biographers, John. The apostle writes: "And when He had taken the Book, the four beasts and four and twenty elders fell down before the Lamb, having every one of them harps, and golden vials full of odors, which are the prayers of saints." ~ Revelation 5:8.

Evidently, as a family of six, we arrived in the United States, in October 1994, having lived in England, throughout our youth and adolescent years. In fact, my four children were born in England. But like a blank sheet of paper, we arrived in America, not being able to open even a bank account. With alarming regularity, we were told that we needed to establish credit in America, as all that we did in England, seemed unavailing.

While the United States is a society that closes the door on you without a high credit rating, the Kingdom of Yahweh is opened by prayer and fasting. Therein, faith is the currency in use. We cannot accept our feelings as a guide for doing what is right, but only as a result of having done what is right!

Therefore, after about a year living in Florida, my husband and I decided that we wanted to purchase a house, but like everything else, we were again told that we did not have any 'credit rating.' Perhaps it might have been considered a fleeting illusion, nevertheless, we pensively went to look at several houses, but no one gave serious consideration to the idea of a mortgage.

In fact, we vividly recall that we had earlier gone to see Charlie, the developer, who was responsible for building the home in which we now live. During that encounter, he made it known to us that he could not help. Therein, our third daughter, who was eleven years old at the time, said to my husband: "Dad, do you really want a house." "He told her yes," she then said, "then we will need to pray and fast." My husband told her, "you set the date." so we yielded to the wise words of our daughter.

She dutifully set the date for the Thursday of that week, as such, all members of the family fasted on that Thursday. The next day, being Friday, my husband said to me, "let's go and see Charlie," whom we had earlier seen about a week ago. There is indeed a difference when one has met scriptural criteria.

As we entered his office, he was on the telephone, speaking to someone. We then waited until he was through talking to the person.

Strangely, as soon as he saw us, he cordially inquired whether we were interested in purchasing a home. Thinking he might have recognized us from an earlier visit, he simply picked us the phone and called the Bank, letting them know that we were interested in a house.

With only one of us working at the time, and two salaries were needed to obtain a mortgage, to the naked eye, it seemed a near impossible task, yet we came fully prayed up.

Therefore, the Bank manager told him to give us directions to the office in Hollywood, Florida. Within half an hour, we were sitting in his office discussing the possibility of a mortgage. And within two hours, we left that Bank with a mortgage, and yes, on the strength of one salary, but by the grace of Yahusha HaMashiah. In fasting the privilege is ours, and the Glory is Yah!

After we came back from the Bank, we went to see Charlie who handed us several keys to pick a house of our choice. And we chose the one that was nearest to completion.

Evidently, we can testify that, as Yahusha had spoken to His disciples about the exercise of faith, "Howbeit this kind goeth not out but by prayer and fasting" (Matthew 17: 21).

Whether it be the purchase of a home, the feeling of being unwell, or the cruel decree of mandated vaccine, we should not fear the giants of our troubled circumstances. But like King David, use prayer and fasting as the sling and stone of our weapons of warfare.

Thus, we are told of Daniel the Prophet: "Now when Daniel knew that the writing was signed, he went into his house; and his windows being open in his chamber toward Jerusalem, he kneeled upon his knees three times a day, and prayed, and gave thanks before his Yah, as he did aforetime" (Daniel 6: 10).

Moreover, as a family of six, we lived in Florida for months without any income, and the steady depletion of that which we had. Due mainly to our waiting the reception of our Green cards, it was indeed a trying time, as funds were running low. Interestingly, one morning we received a letter from the lawyer, wo had been responsible for selling out home in England.

He told us in the letter that during the proceedings, a mistake had been made, in the calculation of the finance, and he was now forwarding the rest of the money to us. It was a time that we really needed it. Yahweh knew ahead of time that we would encounter the hardship in the US, so, He wisely held back part of the money, until the time of our personal and familial famine.

To Yah be the Glory, great things He has done - the privilege has been mine.

Dear Father thank You for your Word, which has been a lamp to my feet and a light to my path, sacred is Your Name Yahweh. Continue to teach me your truth and the faith that will make me stronger. Help Me to be righteous in all my doings. You have given me so much dear Father and because You give me live, I entrust my life to You. Let me be detained in the care of Your love, inspire my mind and heal my infirmities. Help me to prevail by Your grace and mercy. In the Name of Yashua Ha Mashiach. Amen!

Joan Mattocks

His Purpose for My Life

For we are God's handiwork, created in Christ Jesus to do good works, which God prepared in advance for us to do. Eph 2:10

Have you ever thought about questions like, *what is the purpose for my life? Am I living a purpose-driven life? or how do I fulfill my purpose?* I believe each of us was created with a divine purpose to make a positive impact on someone's life. Recently, I have been thinking more about my purpose. Although I have thought about it for a long time, it became more evident during the coronavirus lockdown. I thought about all the people that needed help; the vulnerable, the disenfranchised, women in distress, foster care youth, the homeless, and all the other people who are in need. I also thought about different ways I could engage family members, friends, and colleagues in creating a positive impact in the life of people in need.

One of the things I discussed with family members and friends was to invite women to share their testimonial (s) to encourage and inspire other women all around the globe. I felt that many women were experiencing difficult times and perhaps one testimony could help them develop the faith needed to go on. The goal was that women would share their experiences about God's grace, mercies, faithfulness, and providence in their lives. After making several phone calls and explaining the benefits of the devotional, I was thrilled, excited, and encouraged to proceed. After a few weeks with great encouragement from Sis. Sharon Roberts, I began to receive testimonials from women all over the world. I was blessed in so many ways after reading these testimonies. Women invited other women and today we have 135 testimonials.

I realized early on that an encouraging word, a sincere concern, or a prayer can change the path of a person's life. We were made in God's image for a specific purpose to reflect His love to a hurting world. This remains an important movement for women to become agents of change and identify ways and means to share the love of God by helping others in need.

Eternal Father, thank You for showing me the purpose You have for my life. All I possess have been favored through Your grace. Lead me to generously share this grace to others in need. Thank You for all the women that contributed to this devotional. May it be used as a mean of inspiring and empowering women all around the globe to accept You as their Personal Savior. Help me to continue to walk in my purpose. Refresh, refuel, empower, and encourage us in Your will. Provide the resources needed to continue this important work in Jesus Name. Amen!

Dr. Donna Barrett

2021 Author Biographies

Sausana Abraham was born in Saudi Arabia. Part of her childhood was spent in a Christian boarding school in Kerala, India. On Saturdays, a Christian group taught her about the Bible. One of the songs they sang was "Jesus never fails." This song touched her heart and strengthened her faith. At the age of 10, her dad was jailed for teaching the Word of God. God delivered her father from death/imprisonment after many churches and believers prayed and fasted for him. The power of God was evidenced through this experience and she accepted Jesus as her Savior and was baptized at the age of 13. Jesus has transformed her life.

Ann Marie Troupe-Afflick lives in Canada with her husband and two children. She is a teacher by profession and currently volunteers in the women's ministry and children's ministry departments at her church. She enjoys cooking, reading and nature walks. Her motto is found in Proverbs 3 V 5-6 "Trust in the Lord with all thine heart and lean not unto thine own understanding. In all thy ways acknowledge Him, and He shall direct thy paths."

Looka Albert has been married for six years. Her marriage produced two boys, Logan and Abraham. She is a credit and collection finance specialist for Miami Dade County. She loves the outdoors and spends time with family and friends. Looka believes that if you truly want to live for God, He will make it happen. She started an online ministry named @looksministry that focuses on encouraging believers to live a life pleasing to God to help believers along the way. She looks forward to what the Lord is and going to do in the future.

Judith Alexander hails from Trinidad and Tobago. She and her husband have retired in the Cayman Islands after completing their teaching careers. They have three lovely daughters and two precious granddaughters.

Georgia Alvaranga is an educator who lives in the state of New York. She is very active in her church and serves in the children's ministry and education department. Georgia also enjoys witnessing to others through her singing ministry.

Dr. Elaine M. Barclay is a native of Cleveland, Ohio. She is the second of four children born to God-fearing and loving parents, James, and Lucille Jenkins. God is and will always be the center of her life. Elaine and her husband, Kevin have been married for over 29 years. Their predestined union brought forth four passionate children and three powerful grandsons. Elaine is known to many for her love for Christ, love for family and friends, determined spirit, and the ability to function with resilience when "life," happens. She was given a title of 'water,' meaning no matter what comes, depending on God will overcome the objective and keep moving towards her purpose in this thing we call 'life.' For the past 20 years, she has served the community through providing mental health and spiritual counseling and is an acknowledged relationship expert in following the original intent of marriage. Her phrase is "Building Communities of Unity on Purpose!"

Chante Barrett lives in Miramar, Fl. She has been a real estate agent for the past four years and currently serves as the team lead of The HomeValue Group/Keller Williams. She enjoys reading, going to the beach, and traveling around the world with her family and friends.

Dr. Donna Barrett is a native of Jamaica. Her humble beginnings were saturated with a deep love for God which was displayed every-day in morning and evening worship. Donna and her husband, Philip have been married for over 36 years. Their union produced three beautiful daughters and three amazing grand-children.

Donna is known to many for her giving heart, deep love for family, tenacious spirit, and resilient attitude. She is a devoted wife, mother, sister, aunt, and friend. For the past 30 years she has made her mark as an astute business professional forging relationship with other business professionals to promote homeownership. She is one of the leaders in her local church and is often called to serve in different leadership capacities. She loves to work with young people and is committed to their growth. She is also the CEO/Founder of Fostering Connections, Inc., a non-profit organization with a mission to help people in need.

Nekeisha Basko lives in Atlanta, GA with her husband and two children; Devon and Laila. She has been a registered nurse for over 11 years and currently works from home as a Case Manager. She enjoys home decorating, shopping, and going on vacations with her family. God is her refuge and strength, even in difficult times.

Yvonne Black is a native of Jamaica. She currently lives in Florida. She has three beautiful daughters, Lavinia, Aniska, and Royann, and five amazing grandchildren. She loves the Lord and her faith in Him is strong.

Sonia Black is a dental nurse in Mandeville, Jamaica. She is married and has four children. She is a member of the Seventh-day Adventist Church in Mandeville, Manchester, Jamaica.

Delloris Bleasdell is a native of Jamaica. She currently resides in Florida. She serves in the children's ministry department at her local church.

Debbie Bovell, Ed.D., lives on the sunny island of Barbados. She has served as an educator for the past 32 years. She is married with two adult children. She has served in several capacities including teacher, elder, women's ministries leader, and reading program coordinator. She is passionate about improving the reading proficiency of children on the island so that they can be empowered to serve God and their fellow man more fully.

Michell Buttler is a mother, teacher, and most of all, daughter of God.

Alyssa Clarke is about to enter her junior year of high school and is excited to see where it takes her and all she can accomplish in the name of God. She is working on becoming a polyglot and aspires to be successful in the medical field wherever Christ places her. Her ultimate goal in life is to praise God in all she does and says.

Michele Edwards-Collie *is the President/Founder of The King's Daughter, LLC. Michele has a 30-year career in banking, including branch management and specifically in mortgage financing. During her years of helping over 1000 families achieve the dream of homeownership, she has also taken the time to learn various aspects of budgeting and basic principles that lead to wealth. Her calling is to empower others to grow spiritually, emotionally, and financially – 'To Move from Poverty to Prosperity!' Michele is a graduate of Florida State University and is currently pursuing her Masters in Divinity at Asbury Theological Seminary. She is an author, trainer, motivational speaker, workshop facilitator, and financial coach. She is active with various community service organizations including Delta Sigma Theta Sorority, Inc. Michele's favorite quote and the creed by which she lives her life is "Be the Change you wish to see in the World – Gandhi." Michele is married with three children and lives in Sunrise, Florida.*

***Crystal Dames** born and raised in Nassau, Bahamas is the second of three children to Delbon Johnson and Pearlene Smith. Crystal has been married to her loving husband Kenneth Dames, II for over 13 years. Their union produced two children, Christian and*

Makayla. She enjoys working with young people, singing, acting, and other activities.

Viviene Davis is married to Roderick Davis. Together they have one daughter and a son-in-law and are the proud grandparents of their grandson, Josiah. They reside in Miramar, Florida, and attend Cooper City Church of God.

Dr. Maryse Desir is an educator in the Broward County Public Schools in South Florida for more than 28 years. She has one daughter who is also a teacher in the same county. She is the grandmother of three beautiful children. As a servant of God, she joyfully serves as the head deaconess in her church and loves to share the love of God wherever she goes.

Stephanie Johnson-Dingome is a Visiting Scholar in African History at the University of Alabama. She is happily married to Gill; they have four adult sons and two grandsons. Stephanie divides her time between Paris, France, and Birmingham, Alabama.

Georgia Douglas was born and raised in the Blue Mountains of Jamaica and in her formative years developed a relationship with the Lord through nature. Her early education began at the Minto All-Age School then transitioned to Kingsway High School and the College of Arts Science and Technology, now the University of Technology. Georgia is a divorced mother of two adult daughters who are married and have added two sons to her life and one 5-year-old grandson. She currently works in Healthcare and manages her own business.

Yvonne Edwards holds multiple licenses such as real estate broker, currently working as an associate, 215 licenses to sell life, health, and variable annuities She holds a Masters in Business Administration/ Marketing from the University of Phoenix, a BSC in Education from the University of the West Indies, Mona, Jamaica, and a BA in Elementary Education and Certified Nursing Assistant.

Dr. Sandra Fletcher has been an educator for over 37 years serving students in grades K- college. She is the Dean of Women at Northern Caribbean University, Jamaica, and has been married to Oswald for 38.5 years, during which time they raised three wonderful adult children.

Shantell N.L. Florival is the fifteenth child of Howard and Gloria Lewis. Her mother gave birth to three sets of twins. Married to Eddie Florival for 24 years, she has one stepson Nicarrio Florival, a daughter-in-law, and one granddaughter.

Brenda Ferdinand was born in Trinidad, West Indies, where she was a teacher. She now resides in New Jersey and is enjoying life as a retiree. Though she now lives alone, she never feels lonely because of her faith in God. She takes life one day at a time and trusts God to provide for her present and future needs.

Susan Gay, M.A.Ed., MCHES is originally from Barbados, an island in the southeastern Caribbean. She received her MA in Education in Community Health Education from the University of Alabama at Birmingham. She is also a Master Certified Health Education Specialist. As an island girl, Susan's favorite and happy place is the ocean. She also enjoys writing, traveling, and teaching.

***Susan Gooding-Liburd** is a child of God above all. She is a wife, mother, sister, daughter, and friend. She committed her life to the Lord at the age of 16 and has continued to trust and follow Him and will continue to do so for the rest of her life. Her favorite Bible verses are, **Proverbs 3:5-6** "Trust in the Lord with all your heart and lean not on your own understanding; in all your ways submit to Him, and He will make your paths straight." **Jeremiah 29:11** "For I know the plans I have for you," declares the Lord, "plans to prosper you and not to harm you, plans to give you hope and a future."*

***Dorrett Gonzales** was a registered pediatric nurse for 35 years. She loved her job, caring for children and their families. There is a saying that if you love what you do, then you'll never work a day in your life! Dorrett stated, "that could be her." Now, blessed to be happily retired, she is available to assist family, friends, and neighbors, wherever there is a need. A "church goer" for most of her life, a few years ago had an overwhelming desire to have a more meaningful relationship with God. She rededicated her life to Him and she knows it is the best decision she could have made.*

***Carol Nyack nee Gopaul** is a native of Trinidad and Tobago. She lives in the Cayman Islands with her husband, Pastor Wesley Nyack. She has two sons and daughters-in-law, and one granddaughter. She is also a retired school principal. She worships at the Bodden Town Seventh Day Adventist, Cayman Islands. Her hobbies include swimming, star and moon gazing,* *walking on the beach, baking, and gardening. Carol serves as a Conference and Union School Board member*

Gwendolyn G Greenslade is the third child of Bishop Charles and Patricia Rolle and the mother of four children, one daughter, three sons, and two beautiful granddaughters. Born into a church family, she feels because of her father's status as Bishop, it is safe to say being a PK (preacher's kid) she knows the church and received the baptism of the Holy Ghost at the age of nineteen. Although she had many setbacks and pitfalls, believes God looked beyond her faults and saw her need. She shared, "He picked me up turned me around, placed my feet on solid ground. For years I served as Evangelist and assistant of the women's ministry in my father's church. Then the Lord called me into pastoral ministry." As a pastor of God's House of Praise International, she describes it as a place where miracles happen, and the love of God is demonstrated.

Celeste Gunter is a retiree. She is also a mother and grandmother. She has been a baptized member of the Seventh-day Adventist Church for over 40 years. Presently, she is one of the Elders at the Shelter Rock SDA church in NY. Also, she serves as head Sabbath School Superintendent and assistant to the prayer coordinator. She loves the Lord and desires to make Heaven her home. She believes God hears and answers prayer.

Silvia Ham-Ying MSC., BSC. (Hons), Dip Ed, RN. is a retired health care professional with experience in clinical practice, education, and management. She conducts healthy lifestyle seminars and health checks for churches and the wider community. Silvia is also a wife, a mother, and a grandmother.

Marcia Holness is a retired dental assistant in Mandeville, Jamaica. She is married and has three children.

Faith D. Housen was born in London, England. She is the youngest of five girls born to her deceased parents. She immigrated to the United States when she was a teenager and was an active member of her local Seventh-day Adventist Church in Long Island New York. Her undergraduate studies were at Colombia Union College in Tacoma Park, Maryland, and John Jay University in New York City. She is also a former New York City probation officer. Faith now resides in Florida and lives alone. She holds dear to her heart the early principles of being taught by her mother to love the Lord and to develop an everlasting relationship with Him. In these trying times, Faith holds to Psalms 46:1 "God is our refuge and strength a very present help in the time of trouble" as her life support in sustaining her through each day. Faith's motto for those who walk the Christian pathway is, "hold onto God's unchanging hand, He will never leave you or forsake you."

Claudette Johnson is a management consultant who directs mission-critical business transformation for clients in health care, insurance, financial services, and diversified industries. She is a credential business continuity professional who is well versed in risk management for application development and technology strategy. A proactive leader who advocates for social change, she has a passion for philanthropy which led her to launch Living

Dolls International Ambassadors. This private venture aligns with a few NGOs (Nazkat and IOWD) that promote economic empowerment, health, social and emotional wellbeing of vulnerable populations in at-risk communities.

Kameisha Johnson lives in Atlanta, Georgia with her husband and daughter. She works as a human resource manager in the government-industry. She enjoys spending time with her family and friends, reading, and baking. She loves the Lord and is thankful for His everlasting love. Kameisha believes there is no limit to what God can do and will do. She desires to have spiritual eyes that see beyond what is and a heart that eagerly anticipates God's guidance, goodness, and grace.

Josiane Jones, nee Lancette, was born on the French Caribbean island of Martinique. She grew up in a strictly Catholic family with twelve siblings. She learned not to entertain any conversation about religion with anyone not of her faith. But in 1961, God used her curiosity to bring her into His fold. To this day, she remains the only Seventh-day Adventist in the family. After graduation, she received her calling to work in the Franco-Haitian Union office as Secretary to the President, Pastor James Fulfer. She left Haiti in July 1969 to marry Lester Jones and join him in St. Lucia where they both taught at the St. Lucia SDA Academy. They have two grown sons, Andre and Reuel. Josiane's heart desires that her brothers and sisters will come to the knowledge of the gospel of Jesus Christ and accept it before it is too late. Her hobbies include gardening, cooking, traveling, and sharing literature.

Lorna Moore-Keize was born in the parish of St Catherine, Jamaica. She is a graduate of Mico Teachers College, Jamaica, and the University of Phoenix. She has been married to the love of her life, Alphonso for 39 years and has three adorable daughters. She is the owner/manager of K'S Haven Assisted Living Facility and Cherry Haven. She attends Saving Grace Seventh-day Adventist Church in Hollywood FL.

Debra Johnson-King Debra Johnson-King is the Founder/CEO of The Debjon Group, LLC. (TDG). TDG offers personal and business coaching strategies, specializing in assisting clients in the areas of financial management with an emphasis on personal financial development, debt elimination, homebuyer education services, credit building/rebuilding services, real estate, income protection and/or replacement, and developing multiple streams of income. Debra is very goal-oriented and has an impeccable track record of yielding results and brings over twenty-five years of experience to TDG. Debra speaks regularly at faith-based organizations, empowerment seminars, Fortune 500 Companies, etc., delivering content in these areas. Over the course of her career, she has presented to, coached, counseled, and trained thousands of people in achieving financial independence. Debra holds an MBA, as well as various licenses and certifications

Leteshia Lewis lives in Atlanta, Georgia with her two daughters. She is always cheering her girls on, supporting both in the extra curriculum activities, such as tumbling and cheerleading events. Her youngest is the oldest daughter's biggest supporter in her film major at Georgia State University. She is a strong believer in the

Lord. She believes in trusting the journey God has planned for her life. Her favorite Scripture is found in Proverbs 3:5

"Trust in the Lord with all your heart, and do not lean on your own understanding."

Joan Mattocks was born in Jubilee hospital, Kingston Jamaica; thereafter she spent her formative years in Castleton St. Mary, before migrating to England. Interestingly, her husband also came from St. Mary. She was schooled in a little town called Dudley, within the conurbation of the West Midlands; firstly Woodside Junior school and then Holly Hall Secondary Modern.

After graduating from High School, she went to Bilston College, at the age of 16 and there met her husband. Providentially, they both migrated to England in the same year and lived approximately 7 miles apart. Joan was brought up in a home with her sister and two brothers where they embraced the Seventh-day Sabbath as the Holy Day of rest. She went on to achieve a diploma in Nursing at Sandwell Health Authority (RN). Joan stated "I have been blessed with a Yah Fearing husband who leads his family to the altar daily. I am also blessed with four (4) children and six (6) grandchildren."

Beverley S. Monroe is a native of the beautiful twin-island Republic of Trinidad and Tobago. She loves children and had previously worked within the Seventh-day Adventist School system for approximately 15 years. She enjoys working for Jesus, especially using her God-given talents of planning, and organizing programs, singing, and writing. Beverley has lived in the state of Florida for several years. She presently serves as an ELA and ESL educator, as well as an adjunct lecturer for the Florida International University in the United States of America."

Carmen Palmer is a mother of four children, eight grandchildren, and one great-granddaughter. She is a retired medical assistant. Over the years, she has worked in various medical facilities. Carmen embarked on her new career in real estate and is a proud agent of The HomeValue Group. Her passion for health care was to help people in the medical field. Her passion has transferred to assisting families in securing a home. She is a member of the Saving Grace SDA Church, she serves in various departments.

Marcia Mighty-Powell is a mother of two and a grandmother of two. She is a licensed real estate professional. She stated that it is a joy to make her clients happy as she assists with their choice for their dream home. Marcia has a passion for working with children. She is a reliable leader with a passion to impart to youth the knowledge of God. She serves as an assistant to the Florida Conference Master Guide trainer. She is also a Sabbath schoolteacher and an assistant Adventist youth leader in her local church. Her true purpose is to be of service to others.

Aldyth Roach is a retired echo sonographer who remains actively involved as a caretaker and homemaker, serving her family and church in Florida with the tender devotion to her belief that Jesus manifested His ministry on earth. She quotes Ellen G. White, "He showed His sympathy for them, ministered to their needs and won their confidence. Then he bade them, "Follow me." Aldyth still manages to find time for gardening and delights in floral and gift basket arrangements.

Sharon Roberts has been working in the medical field for the past 16 years and enjoys geriatric nursing. Her hobbies are cooking, entertaining, and reading. She also has a deep passion for women's ministries and is currently an integral part of her husband's ministry as he serves as Senior Pastor for two churches in the Florida Conference of Seventh-day Adventists.

Pastor Smythe-Forbes is a graduate of Northern Caribbean University (NCU), where she pursued a BA in Theology and a minor in Youth Ministry. Upon graduation in 1998 she began serving as a missionary for the General Conference of Seventh-day Adventist in South Korea. In 2004, she became the chaplain of Victor Dixon High School. As a chaplain, she taught religious education classes to young people in grades 9-12. In May 2011, Pastor Smythe-Forbes completed a MA in Pastoral Studies with a concentration in Church Development, at Oakwood University. From 2010-2011 she served faithfully as the Pastor of Administration at Madison Mission Seventh Day Adventist Church. She currently serves as the district pastor in the Asia District of Churches in South Manchester. The district is comprised of six churches and the Campbell's Castle Preparatory School. She believes that God has given her the vision to create a church model that employs creative revolutionary methods for church growth. She is excited to announce the good news of the Gospel of Jesus Christ. She is confident that God will bring to fruition His driven purposes. She is married to Egerton Forbes and together they have five children, Jaden, Azriel, Talia, Jamario, and Lamario.

Marcia Scott is a student nurse. She is married and a mother of six children and six grandchildren. She is a praying cheerful woman.

Florence Sinclair is a Jamaican residing in the United States of America. Her area of specialty is early childhood education. She has a passion to teach others how to trust in the Lord. She is thankful to God for the opportunity to help others in need.

Iska Stoddart is a graduate student and aspiring health professional. She has served as a church organist and pianist for 15 years. In her spare time, she enjoys crocheting and composing songs.

Terry-Ann Talbert has been an educator in Miami Dade County Public School District for five years where she found her passion for teaching. Outside of the classroom, she enjoys simply serving those around her. She stated, "I have many things in my life that I am proud of, but what I hold in the highest regard is the robust faith that walking the Lord has cultivated in me over the years." It was not easy! I cried some tears that I never thought I had. But guess what, in the end, I saw the refiners' fire made me stronger and better for it! God is good!"

Alexandira Espeut-Thompson hails from the parish of Kingston, Jamaica but if you ask her, she was an island hopper-from Kingston to St. Elizabeth to St. Ann. Currently, a mother of one God-sent son via a blessed husband, she is a slowly transforming introvert. She loves to read, write, draw/design, and connecting with God through nature. Her prayer is that as she grows in Christ, she will be a better example for the people around her.

***Bula Rose Haughton-Thompson** is a trained Bible Worker and a member of the Goshen Seventh-day Adventist Church in West Jamaica Conference. She is committed to her Lord and the Seventh-day Adventist Church. This year she and Norman are celebrating twenty-five years of wedded bliss.*

***Christine Thompson** is a school library support technician for a school board in Ontario, Canada. She enjoys discussing and studying the Bible as well as creative arts.*

***Louise Watson-Tomlin** is a Dental Practitioner with over thirty years of experience. She and her husband are parents to four adult sons, three daughters-in-law, and one precious granddaughter. As a practicing Christian who gave her life to Christ 30 years ago, her passion is to serve the less fortunate in whatever way she can until Christ returns.*

***Jean Trotman** has been an educator for more than 40 years. She loves God and people and delights in reading the Word and the Spirit of Prophecy. She has been married to Al for 32 years and they have a son, Zachary. Jean lives on the beautiful island of Barbados. She has served her church in many capacities but is currently the Sabbath School Superintendent. She has held this post for the last 12 years.*

***Annette L. Vaughan** is originally from the Caribbean Island of Barbados. She currently resides in the Cayman Islands with her* *husband, Bentley. Annette recently retired from the teaching profession after a total of 38 years of service in both countries. Annette enjoys traveling, writing, reading, photography, vegetarian cooking, and homemaking. She and her husband share their passion for music ministry with their local church in the Cayman Islands.*